OPPORTUNITIES

in

Metalworking Careers

D1358180

OPPORTUNITIES
in

Metalworking
Careers

REVISED EDITION

MARK ROWH

New York   Chicago   San Francisco   Lisbon   London   Madrid   Mexico City
Milan   New Delhi   San Juan   Seoul   Singapore   Sydney   Toronto

The *McGraw·Hill* Companies

Library of Congress Cataloging-in-Publication Data

Rowh, Mark.
    Opportunities in metalworking careers / By Mark Rowh. — Rev. ed.
       p.   cm.
    ISBN 0-07-149310-7 (alk. paper)
    1. Metal-work—Vocational guidance.   I. Title.

  TS213.R694   2008
  671.023—dc22   2007047021

1 2 3 4 5 6 7 8 9 10 11 12 13 14 15 16 17 18 19 20 DOC/DOC 0 9 8

ISBN 978-0-07-149310-9
MHID   0-07-149310-7

Interior design by Rattray Design

McGraw-Hill books are available at special quantity discounts to use as premiums and sales promotions or for use in corporate training programs. To contact a representative, please visit the Contact Us pages at www.mhprofessional.com.

This book is printed on acid-free paper.

This book is dedicated to Rowh 1.0: Linda, Lisa, David, and Jenny, and to all the wonderful additions to the family since publication of the first edition of this book.

CONTENTS

Foreword   xi
Acknowledgments   xv
Introduction   xvii

1. **Metal, Metal Everywhere**   1

   Importance of metalworking. Metalworking through
   the ages. Benefits of a career in metalworking. More
   exploration.

2. **Many Dimensions of Metalworking**   11

   Metalworking fields. Varied career options.

3. **Sheet-Metal Working**   17

   Position titles. A day on the job. Working conditions.
   Right skills. Getting trained. Key questions.

4. **Machining and Machine Operation**   29

Work performed by machinists. Roles of machine operators. Related job titles. Working conditions. Getting trained. Many options.

5. **Structural and Reinforcing Metalworking**   41

Typical duties. Related job titles. Working conditions. Right skills. Getting trained.

6. **Welding**   49

Types of welding. Multiple roles. Tasks performed. Related job titles. What it takes. Working conditions. Getting trained.

7. **Jewelry Making**   65

What jewelers do. Creative angle. Related job titles. Career pluses. Getting trained.

8. **Training Options**   73

Apprenticeships. On-the-job training. Government-sponsored training programs. Programs offered by schools and colleges. Financing your training. Obtaining financial aid.

9. **Earnings, Benefits, and Career Opportunities**   89

Earning potential. Fringe benefits. Employment prospects. Opportunities for women and minorities. Career possibilities for the disabled.

10. Planning for the Future   **97**

Locating job openings. Doing well in interviews.

Appendix A: Schools and Colleges Offering
    Metalworking Programs   101
Appendix B: Selected Organizations Related to
    Metalworking   147
Further Reading   153

FOREWORD

DO YOU LIKE CARS? How about music? Do you surf the Web? Do you play sports? How about watching DVDs? Is bling your thing?

From cars to guitars, bikes to bracelets, computers to the chair you're sitting on, these products have at least two things in common—you or someone you know comes in contact with them daily, and they're all manufactured with components made through metalworking processes. What is metalworking, you might ask? This book will answer that question in detail. Suffice it to say that metalworking includes a wide range of processes that cut, shape, form, bend, join, drill, or punch metal for application in countless products that add convenience and enjoyment to our lives.

Why should you care about metalworking? Because you are about to embark on a career, and you want to make sure you select an occupation that will provide not only security and stability but also enjoyment and satisfaction. As you consider a career choice, why not take a good look at metalworking, where there is an abundance of different jobs covering a wide range of skills and requiring various degrees of training and education?

Metalworking is performed at thousands of companies throughout the country. These include every kind of company—from large automotive, appliance, medical, construction, aircraft, and electronic equipment makers with thousands of employees each and whose names are familiar to everyone, to the small shop down the street with fewer than ten workers providing fulfillment for those with an entrepreneurial spirit. Regardless of the size of the company, the skills and knowledge required of workers in the metalworking industry are learned through a combination of classroom instruction and hands-on experience. And there are nationally recognized credentials you can achieve through the National Institute for Metalworking Skills that provide potential employers with documentation of your skills and to certify that you can get the job done.

If you have good mathematics and analytical skills and computer skills, enjoy making things with your hands and thinking creatively, and the imagination to envision what can be made, a career in metalworking may be your passport to success. Metalworkers learn and hone their skills through hands-on training, practical experience, and classroom learning. Many learn a trade through formal apprenticeships. And classroom learning can lead to associate, bachelor's, and graduate degrees in engineering technology or management. Jobs in the metalworking industry provide real opportunity for advancement and financial success. It is not uncommon for people to work their way up from the shop floor to the ranks of management or even ownership.

Metalworking companies throughout the North America face a skills gap, as many skilled employees are nearing retirement. These companies seek to hire men and women who have the right mixture of mechanical aptitude, can-do attitude, basic skills and knowledge, and the desire to learn more. Looking to get started? Stop by a local manufacturer or community/technical college or call one of the many metalworking trade associations and ask them about career opportunities in precision metalworking. It could be the visit or call that opens a whole new world of opportunities for you.

David C. Sansone
Executive Director
Precision Metalforming Association Educational Foundation

Acknowledgments

The author greatly appreciates the cooperation of the following organizations in the development of this book:

American Welding Society
International Association of Machinists and Aerospace
    Workers
National Institute for Metalworking Skills
National Tooling and Machining Association
North American Die Casting Association
Precision Metalforming Association
RWM
Tooling and Manufacturing Association

Some material also has been derived from the *Occupational Outlook Handbook*, 2006–2007 edition, published by the U.S. Department of Labor.

INTRODUCTION

CHOOSING A CAREER is one of life's most important decisions. Naturally, for any potential occupation, you should ask plenty of questions, including the following: What are the long-term expectations that workers will continue to be needed in the field? What kind of earning potential does the field offer? What approaches, skills, or special training will be needed to gain employment in the first place, as well as to succeed once hired? What tasks will be performed in carrying out the responsibilities of the job? What kind of job advancement is available?

When it comes to a possible career in metalworking, the future holds significant promise. After all, metals are among the most basic materials used by human beings. People who build or repair metal goods or structures play an important role in our society. This has been true for many years and should continue into the future. Even though advances in technology have introduced new materials such as plastics and ceramics, metals will still be vital in the new century.

Given the continued importance of metal, jobs involved in working with it will continue to hold their own importance. The information provided here should prove helpful to anyone interested in pursuing a related career.

1

METAL, METAL EVERYWHERE

ONE OF THE hallmarks of a civilized society is the ability to make things out of metal. For primitive men and women, implements made of wood and stone were state-of-the-art. But modern people enjoy the use of a variety of materials from which tools, homes, factories, and other structures are built. And no single substance is more necessary than metal.

Importance of Metalworking

Just think about it. All around you, devices and structures made of metal play a key role in your life. Here are just a few examples:

- Schools, houses, apartments, factories, and office buildings contain pipes, reinforcing rods, beams, and many other components made of metal.
- Cars, trucks, and buses are made in large part of steel, aluminum, and other metals.

1

- Various household appliances, from refrigerators to washers and dryers, are built from components that include metal.
- Airplanes, ships, trains, as well as other forms of transportation include large quantities of metal in their construction.
- Today's large bridges would be impossible to build without metal.

Even the tools used to build the items described above are themselves made primarily of metal.

With the widespread use of metals as basic construction materials, the ability to work with them is a highly useful commodity. Persons who can cut, shape, fasten, or otherwise fashion metal parts into useful objects fill a variety of interesting positions.

Metalworking may consist of the construction of anything from jewelry to skyscrapers. It can be a simple process involving a few pieces of basic equipment or a highly technical effort making use of microprocessors and precise measurements. In some cases, the work performed will be the repair of existing items rather than the creation of new ones. Whatever the ultimate goal, metalworking requires special skills. This means that men and women who have developed these skills are needed by various types of employers. With the importance that different metals continue to have as building and repair materials, the work of trained metalworkers represents a promising career area.

Metalworking Through the Ages

Efforts to work with metal have a long and fascinating history. For thousands of years, the ability to create and use metal has been crucial to the development of human society. Historians have even used advances in such technology to label different eras such as the Bronze Age and Iron Age.

Prehistory

Long before modern civilization developed, the first human beings learned to use a variety of materials for tools, weapons, and other purposes. For example, prehistoric men and women chipped one stone against another to create a sharp edge for scraping hides or cutting apart animal carcasses. They developed the ability to make knives, arrowheads, spearheads, and other useful items in a similar fashion. Sometimes they used not only stone but also other available substances, such as bone or wood. The first spear was probably nothing more than a sharpened stick, eventually enhanced by adding a point or head of a harder substance such as stone. What many generations of primitive people did not have, however, was metal.

No one in prehistoric times knew how to extract metal from ores or how to melt it, shape it, or otherwise work with any type of it. Technology was limited to materials that were less durable, less malleable, or both. A piece of stone could be chipped and shaped to some extent, but the possibilities for using it were limited. The same was true of wood and other building materials.

Discovery of Metals

When human beings discovered metals and how to work with them, things changed dramatically. Probably the first to gain widespread use was copper, which is one of the softest and most easily worked metals. It seemed ideal for creating simple tools such as cooking utensils, bracelets, necklaces, and other items. Other soft metals, such as gold and silver, also were found to be easily formed into objects such as jewelry or figurines for artistic or religious uses.

As time passed, these early people who worked with metal began to experiment with both materials and techniques. For example, they learned to combine two or more metals into a new material having different qualities than either of the original, separate metals. Combining copper with tin produced bronze, a metal that gained widespread use for purposes ranging from body armor to domestic utensils.

Once people began to use metal widely, they found it provided enormous advantages. Warriors equipped with metal shields and spears often held the upper hand in battle. Metal knives, axes, and other tools also proved highly effective for more peaceful uses. All in all, the ability to work with various metals became an important element of every civilization.

Over thousands of years, the variety and quality of work with metal increased in many different ways. Probably the most important advancement was the discovery of iron and steel. From ancient Roman times through the Middle Ages and into the present day, iron and steel have played an integral role in human technological development. In everything from agriculture to transportation, these strong and versatile metals have provided essential building materials.

Other metals such as aluminum and lead also have proven important as scientists, technicians, and workers in a wide range of fields have developed ways to manufacture and use them. Virtually every civilized society from ancient times to the present has made wide use of whatever metals were available at the time.

The Industrial Revolution

Many of the most significant developments in metalworking occurred during the Industrial Revolution of the 1700s and 1800s. During this time, the practice of mass production was initiated and expanded, and more and more metal objects were introduced into everyday life.

Some of the most important influences on the continued development of metalworking practices and techniques have included the following:

- Growth of railroads, which required hundreds of thousands of miles of tracks as well as metal components for the trains themselves
- Advances in military technology, with increasingly sophisticated weapons and weapons systems demanding new and improved uses of various metals and alloys
- Invention of the automobile and the subsequent production of untold billions of components for the cars, trucks, and other vehicles that have been produced in the last century
- Growth of large cities and the tall buildings made necessary by limitations in available building space
- Expansion of modern highway systems, including thousands of bridges ranging from small structures to giant spans such as the Golden Gate Bridge
- Recent advances in the air and space industry, the development of nuclear power plants, and other high-tech industries in which metalworkers have faced new challenges and opportunities

Benefits of a Career in Metalworking

Why might anyone pursue a career in a metalworking field? Here are several possible benefits.

Attractive Wages

In general, men and women employed in metalworking jobs earn attractive wages and benefits. Their jobs require special skills, and employers are willing to pay wages reflecting the particular knowledge and skills involved. In the more complex positions, workers may earn several times the average pay received by unskilled workers. In addition, metalworkers often receive substantial fringe benefits. These benefits may include pension plans, health insurance, medical insurance, educational pay, and other valuable forms of enhancement and support.

Job Satisfaction

A good job should offer more than just good wages. It should also prove interesting. Many people find that metalworking jobs challenge them to learn new skills and then apply them in the process of construction, repair, or other workplace efforts.

Unfortunately, many workers in what are often called unskilled jobs find little satisfaction in their work. Many such jobs in agriculture, service industries, and other areas require no special training or abilities, thus virtually anyone can perform them. However, they usually pay low wages and often consist of boring, repetitive work.

Most jobs in metalworking, on the other hand, are different. They can be done only by people who have mastered certain basic techniques and who in many cases have completed special training. As a result, workers who have developed such specialized capabilities can experience justifiable compensation and self-confidence. And perhaps even more important, the end result is often a product of which the worker can be proud. The act of building or repairing something can be extremely rewarding. One of the nicest feelings in life is to step back and take a long look at a building, bridge, or piece of equipment that you have built or helped construct. Persons employed in metalworking usually can enjoy the tangible benefits of such accomplishments.

Suitable Work Environment

Do you want to spend your working life seated behind a desk in an air-conditioned office? If so, a metalworking job may not be for you. On the other hand, if you would prefer working with your hands in an active and potentially varied environment, perhaps working as a machinist, welder, or other metalworker will be just right for you.

This working environment may consist of a workbench in a small business, the floor of a large factory, the unfinished portion of a bridge or skyscraper, or any number of other settings. It may be indoors or out. Some jobs will involve going from one construction site to the next as projects are completed. Others may be on the production line of a huge plant or in the workroom of a small one. In any case, the surroundings and the type of work undertaken may be well suited to your own particular idea of an appropriate workplace.

Job Opportunities Without Four Years of College

You don't need a bachelor's degree to pursue a career in metalworking. Instead, you can participate in on-the-job training or an apprenticeship, or you can enroll in a program taking anywhere from a few months to two years to complete, depending on the field involved and the type of training followed.

In some cases, you can go straight from high school to a metalworking job. In others, a comprehensive training effort will be needed. But in either situation, you can find yourself in a well-paying job while friends and acquaintances are still in their third or fourth year of postsecondary education.

Geographical Flexibility

Jobs in various metalworking fields can be found throughout the United States, Canada, and many other countries. Of course more positions can be expected in urban areas than rural ones, but there are no special geographical limitations for careers in this field.

This flexibility often can mean finding a good job without having to leave the area where you now live, if that is your preference. If you hope to move to new locations, metalworking skills can be a great asset for helping you find employment in a new area. Because of the widespread use of metal for so many purposes, job possibilities in the various related fields can be found virtually anywhere.

Potential for the Future

When you choose a career, how do you know that there will still be a demand for that kind of work ten years or more into the future? After all, we live in an increasingly changing world. New inventions and entire new industries seem to spring up overnight, and workers are sometimes lost in the transition.

It would be misleading to say that this will never happen in any given technical field, for no one can predict the future with any real degree of accuracy. But the future in many metalworking jobs seems solid. The need for trained metalworkers is expected to continue far into the future, despite the increased use of plastics, ceramics, and other products. Changing technology is unlikely to eliminate the use of metal but may instead prompt new ways of using different metals in combination with other materials.

More Exploration

Want to know more? The following chapters cover various fields within the overall career area of metalworking, along with tips on breaking into the field of your choice and what you can expect if you become employed in this area. Chapter 2 provides an overview of the major metalworking fields. Chapter 3 covers working with sheet-metal, while machining and machine operation are covered in Chapter 4. Chapter 5 looks at structural and reinforcing metalworking, and Chapter 6 provides an introduction to welding. Chapter 7 covers the jewelry-making field.

A look at the educational work needed to prepare for a metalworking career appears in Chapter 8. This chapter also provides tips for doing well in training programs. Chapter 9 discusses earnings and fringe benefits. Approaches to breaking into a metalworking field are covered in Chapter 10. The book also has two appendixes, including a list of schools providing appropriate training programs.

Perhaps a career in metalworking holds promise for you. Take a look at the information provided, and you may find yourself on the way to a promising and worthwhile career.

2

Many Dimensions of Metalworking

Metalworking is a technology that has existed for thousands of years, but it remains one of the most vital aspects of modern life. Methods of working with metal include both traditional practices perfected over the centuries and exciting new techniques developed in today's age of computers and sophisticated industrial applications.

Metalworking Fields

Persons who work with metal hold a wide variety of jobs. Most of them can be grouped into the following major fields:

- Sheet-metal working
- Machining and machine operation
- Structural and reinforcing metalworking

- Welding
- Jewelry making

A brief description of each field follows. Additional details for these occupations are provided in subsequent chapters.

Sheet-Metal Working

Sheet-metal workers make, install, or repair items with sheet metal. They are employed throughout the United States and Canada in a variety of industries. Many of them work in building construction, where they construct hangars, storage buildings, or other structures. Others may install aluminum siding, skylights, roofs, or outdoor signs. Still others work with air-conditioning, heating, or ventilation systems. This work may include fabricating, installing, or repairing air ducts in homes, office buildings, or other structures.

Persons employed in this field sometimes specialize in a specific task, such as installing rain gutters or aluminum siding. They work for various types of employers including large construction companies, smaller firms, and specialized companies providing air-conditioning and heating services. Depending on the type of work being conducted, they may work primarily with hand tools or may use automated equipment.

Machining and Machine Operation

Machinists and machine operators produce precision parts of metal, or sometimes plastic, for a wide range of uses. The items that they produce usually must meet very detailed specifications for size, shape, and other characteristics. For example, machinists and related workers may make parts for airplanes, automobiles, or industrial machinery.

Machinists are highly skilled workers. The main distinction between machinists and machine operators is that machinists concentrate on making or repairing items that must be produced individually or in small quantities, as opposed to those made through assembly lines or other mass production processes. Machine operators, on the other hand, usually produce items in larger quantities where mass production is the goal.

Machinists may work with a wide range of metals including steel, copper, iron, aluminum, and various alloys. The work often involves building or adjusting parts of equipment that must meet specific requirements for size, configuration, or other characteristics. Machinists may build new parts from printed designs, duplicate parts, develop variations of existing items, or make precision repairs.

Machine operators concentrate on high-volume production. They often work in manufacturing plants where they produce items such as parts for various types of equipment and consumer goods.

Structural and Reinforcing Metalworking

Workers in this field are most commonly referred to as *ironworkers*. Their jobs usually consist of assembling the steel or iron frameworks of bridges, buildings, and other large structures. Ironworkers install metal bars, rods, beams, columns, and other components. They may build the internal structure around which a multistory office building is erected, put together reinforcing for a concrete retaining wall, or install steel fire escapes or stairs, among other duties.

This work often involves lifting and positioning steel beams and similar items through the use of derricks or cranes. A typical job might include setting up such equipment, unloading and stacking steel beams, and then hoisting them high into the air as part of a major construction project.

Ironworkers hold jobs across the United States and Canada wherever construction projects are under way. They are more likely to find jobs in growing urban areas.

Welding

Welders join metals together using heat or other special processes. They work in many industries including the construction of ships, airplanes, and automobiles. They also join steel rods and beams in highways, bridges, buildings, and other heavy construction.

Welders may perform any of several basic processes. In electric arc welding, an electric current creates heat as it arcs between the tip of a welding electrode and metal. In gas welding, heat formed by burning gases is used to melt metal and cause it to fuse. In resistance welding, electric current flows through weld metal and heats it. Some welders may perform new types of welding that utilize laser beams or electron beams.

Some persons employed in this field master a variety of welding processes, while others concentrate on a single technique or welding application. Welding jobs in heavy construction or repair of machines and equipment may require specialized skills, but some positions consist of working on an assembly line and using welding machines that make the operator's job less complex.

Welders find a demand for their skills in large corporations, small companies, and a variety of geographical locations throughout North America.

Jewelry Making

Not all metalworking jobs involve construction or heavy manufacturing. The field of making or repairing jewelry offers a different range of opportunities.

Jewelers and related workers perform highly skilled and detailed work. They produce or repair various types of jewelry such as rings, brooches, bracelets, earrings, and necklaces. This work may include working with precious metals such as gold and silver as well as other valuable materials including diamonds and precious and semi-precious gems.

Jewelers may work in manufacturing facilities that specialize in the production of jewelry, in department stores, or in small retail stores. Their work might include anything from assembling a set of earrings to repairing the broken clasp of a necklace. In some instances, their work may cross into other areas such as customer relations or business management.

Because of society's continuing demand for beautiful jewelry, a corresponding demand exists for persons to work in this area. The jewelry-making field offers long-term potential for persons who can perform the precise and often creative work required.

Varied Career Options

Metalworking offers a great deal of variety. A career in this area might take you to the top of a forty-story building where huge steel beams are being hoisted into place. Or it might involve sitting at a workbench assembling a necklace or refining a precision part of a piece of industrial equipment. Such diversity means that many options await the person who hopes to pursue a career in one of these interesting fields.

3

SHEET-METAL WORKING

ONE OF THE most common applications of metalworking technology is forming metal into sheets that can then be used in building all kinds of products. Those who work with this process may be known by a variety of job titles, but the most common overall term is simply *sheet-metal workers.*

Men and women employed as sheet-metal workers in the United States and Canada perform work such as the following:

- Forming and installing rain gutters on houses or other buildings
- Fabricating or installing ducts for air-conditioning systems, heating units, and ventilation systems
- Installing aluminum siding on residences and office buildings
- Making and installing outdoor signs
- Repairing various structures made of sheet metal

Such tasks often include a combination of functions. Sheet-metal workers may assemble items, install them, or do both. They also may provide maintenance and repair services. The U.S. Department of Labor has provided this job description of a sheet-metal worker:

Plans, lays out, fabricates, assembles, installs, and repairs sheet metal parts, equipment, and products, utilizing knowledge of working characteristics of metallic and nonmetallic materials, machining, and layout techniques, using hand tools, power tools, machines, and equipment. Reads and interprets blueprints, sketches, or product specifications to determine sequence and methods of fabricating, assembling, and installing sheet metal products. Selects gauge and type of sheet metal, such as galvanized iron, copper, steel, or aluminum, or nonmetallic material, such as plastics or fiberglass, according to product specifications. Lays out and marks dimensions and reference lines on material, using scribers, dividers, squares, and rulers, applying knowledge of shop mathematics and layout techniques to develop and trace patterns of product or parts . . . or using templates. Sets up and operates fabricating machines, such as shears, brakes, presses, forming rolls, and routers, to cut, bend, block and form, or straighten materials. Shapes metal material over anvil, block, or other form, using hand tools. Trims, files, grinds, deburrs, buffs, and smoothes surfaces, using hand tools and portable power tools. Welds, solders, bolts, rivets, screws, clips, caulks, or bonds component parts to assemble products, using hand tools, power tools, and equipment. Installs assemblies in supportive framework according to blueprints, using hand tools, power tools, and lifting and handling devices. Inspects assemblies and installation for conformance to specifications, using measuring instruments, such as calipers, scales, dial indicators, gauges, and micrometers. Repairs and maintains sheet metal products. May operate computer-aided-drafting (CAD) equipment to develop scale drawings of product or sys-

tem. May operate laser-beam cutter . . . or plasma arc cutter . . .
to cut patterns from sheet metal.

As can be seen by this comprehensive description, sheet-metal
workers may perform a variety of tasks. In fact, they can hold any
of a number of job roles.

Position Titles

Many persons employed in this field hold specialized positions in
which they perform specific types of sheet-metal work. Representative job titles listed by the U.S. Department of Labor in this area
include the following.

Assembler, production line
Assembler, unit
Channel installer
Door-lock installer
Fabricator, shower doors and panel
Fireproof-door assembler
Frame assembler
Hardware installer
Inspector and tester
Kick-plate installer
Measurer
Metal-door assembler
Metal screen, storm door, and window builder
Metal window-screen assembler
Ornamental-metalwork designer
Ornamental metalworker

Screen-frame enameler
Screen installer
Scroll-machine operator
Shop supervisor
Supervisor, assembly department
Supervisor, grinding and spraying

A Day on the Job

For an example of work performed in this field, consider a typical day put in by Kevin, who works for a growing business specializing in heating and air-conditioning systems. His latest job consists of installing such a system in a new building designed to house an auto-repair shop. Not only will the comfort of workers and customers depend on the new system, but safety also will be a key factor: the job will include placing exhaust ducts in several locations so that carbon monoxide and other harmful gases will not accumulate within the building.

To get started, Kevin reviews blueprints that have been provided by his supervisor. Working inside a shop at the company's downtown location, he begins assembling ducts by using computerized equipment purchased recently by his company. This includes a saw that cuts metal according to preprogrammed instructions that Kevin enters electronically. After the ducts have been assembled, Kevin travels by truck to the site of the new building, where he uses hand tools to put the ducts in place. He fastens pieces together and then inspects the system to make sure all parts fit together properly. If necessary, he will make adjustments on-site or take materials back to the shop for adjustments.

In this particular case, the job will take slightly more than one day to complete. Kevin will work an eight-hour day, taking time off for lunch and two short breaks, and at the end of the day he will clean up the area where he has worked, store tools in the truck, and return to the shop for a new assignment.

Specific tasks performed by Kevin or other sheet-metal workers may include the following:

- Using rulers, tapes, or other similar devices to measure material
- Planning layouts for installation projects
- Making calculations by hand or with electronic calculators
- Using small hand tools such as hammers, drills, snips, and hacksaws
- Operating welding machines or soldering equipment
- Operating computer-controlled saws, presses, or other high-tech equipment
- Installing systems and metal parts at sites away from the shop or place of employment
- Altering or repairing structures constructed of sheet metal
- Cutting large metal sheets into smaller pieces
- Fastening materials together with bolts, screws, clips, rivets, or other items
- Checking the size and shape of metal parts for a good fit
- Testing or adjusting completed projects
- Making cost estimates
- Ordering or purchasing materials
- Transporting materials and equipment to job sites
- Communicating with customers and coworkers

Job duties can vary widely within this field. One person may spend all of his or her time assembling products of the same type, such as covers/tops for pick-up trucks or home storage buildings. Another may perform different types of tasks depending upon the needs of each customer or varying assignments from a supervisor.

In working with sheet metal, the overall situation for any one individual may be quite different from that of another. At the same time, the similarity in basic skills used means that workers in this field can sometimes switch from one type of work to another rather easily until they find the situation they like best.

Working Conditions

An advantage of many jobs in the sheet-metal field is that they provide variety in work settings. A job installing heating and air-conditioning ducts, for example, might take an individual to a wide range of different locations. A week or more might be spent at a large office building, followed by a day's work at a private residence. During the course of a year, some workers might experience dozens or even hundreds of changes in work settings. This can be an asset for people who become bored easily and thrive on change.

Not all jobs in the field provide such a degree of change. Some positions involve working in a shop or factory where sheet-metal products are manufactured or assembled. Workers in these kinds of positions show up at the same location every day and encounter relatively little change in working environment. This can be an advantage or disadvantage, depending on personal preferences.

Sheet-metal workers often perform their work outdoors. This can mean enjoying the pleasure of a sunny spring day or suffering the discomfort of winter winds or summer heat. Indoor situations also can be uncomfortable at times—for example, working in a building that has not yet had heating or air-conditioning installed. Workers who encounter such situations learn to compensate by wearing appropriate clothing.

Depending on the environment and the tasks at hand, the work may also involve physical challenges. Actions such as lifting, bending, squatting, or climbing may be a routine part of the job.

Right Skills

Few special skills are absolutely necessary for any person to have the potential to become a sheet-metal worker. Most of the techniques involved can be learned by anyone who has reasonably good hand-to-eye coordination and a basic ability to work with tools. In addition, it helps to have most or all of the following traits:

• **An aptitude for working with mechanical devices.** This might be indicated by aptitude tests as well as past experiences. A person who is good at working on cars, doing carpentry, or repairing household appliances, for instance, probably can learn the basics of sheet-metal working very readily. However, someone who has had no experience in any related activities might nevertheless have the necessary potential.

• **Physical dexterity.** Most of the work in this field requires nimble hands and fingers. A lack of physical strength can perhaps be offset by other skills, but it would be very difficult to perform if you are unable to use your hands easily and efficiently. Also, the ability to climb, crawl, and otherwise move about would be an asset.

• **Stamina.** Persons working with sheet metal may spend all day on their feet in different types of settings, such as a shop with a concrete floor or outdoors during cold weather. The stamina to undertake such work is a necessary commodity.

• **Pride in work skills.** To succeed on a long-term basis, a certain element of pride in doing a good job is needed. This means caring enough to take extra time if necessary or redoing a piece of work that is not up to par. Sheet-metal work requires an eye for precision and a positive working attitude.

Getting Trained

There are a number of ways to learn the basics of sheet-metal working. You do not need to attend college to break into the field, although a high school diploma may be required.

Some vocational schools at the high school level teach basic skills that can be applied to the tasks performed by sheet-metal workers. Still other skills can be learned on your own as you work in a home shop or other setting. In addition, some nonunion employers will hire inexperienced men and women and then train them on the job in an informal fashion.

A more organized and comprehensive approach is to sign up for an apprenticeship program. Such programs are sponsored by the Sheet Metal Workers' International Association (a major union for workers in this field representing approximately 150,000 workers in the United States and Canada) and the Sheet Metal and Air Conditioning Contractors' National Association. They combine work experience and classroom training, normally spread over a four-year period.

Typically, anyone who undertakes a formal apprenticeship program signs an agreement that stipulates his or her responsibilities and rights under the program. Participants then complete at least four years of on-the-job training—about eight thousand working hours—as well as additional time in class.

Some community colleges and postsecondary trade schools offer programs that prepare students for work in this field. As just one example, Algonquin College in Ottawa, Ontario, offers a twenty-four-week program to help prepare sheet metal workers. Structured as a certificate program, it covers the techniques used to design, assemble, and install shop fabricated parts. The program also fulfills the in-school requirements of a formal apprenticeship program. Because it is connected with an apprenticeship program, students must be working in the field when they begin the college program. The latter consists of three eight-week portions, during which students attend classes thirty hours per week. About a third of class time is spent in the shop learning practical hands-on skills. Topics covered include blueprint reading, pattern development, trade calculations, sheet metal (theory), sheet metal (practical), and welding.

Additional examples include programs such as those offered by Southwestern Illinois College at Belleville, Illinois, where students can earn either a certificate or an associate degree in industrial metalworking. In these programs, students learn about making sheet-metal forms and fittings, employing proper layout and construction procedures, and understanding the basics of blueprint reading, welding, and metallurgy. Graduates find jobs in a variety of settings including maintenance groups of manufacturing plants, installation work on construction projects, and installing HVAC (heating, ventilation, and air-conditioning) systems.

Selected course offerings (including related courses outside of metalworking) include the following, which are typical of these fields:

Industrial Math
Industrial Sheet Metal I

Mechanical Blueprint Reading I
Rhetoric and Composition I
Industrial Metallurgy I
Industrial Sheet Metal II
Industrial Welder I
Industrial Sheet Metal III
Mechanical Blueprint Reading II
Industrial Sheet Metal IV
Electives

Other schools offer similar instruction, although sheet-metal programs are not as common as those in some fields, such as machine tool technology. For more details about a given program, access the school's website or review a copy of the course catalog.

Key Questions

The National Training Fund for the Sheet Metal and Air Conditioning Industry has posed these questions for anyone considering a career as a sheet-metal worker:

- Have you finished or are you about to finish high school?
- Did you do well in your math course(s)?
- Did you take drafting and enjoy it?
- Do you like shop work and doing things with your hands?
- Are you willing to work and also go to school?
- Are you healthy, with no major disability and no fear of heights or climbing?
- Would you be willing to work outdoors in varying weather conditions as well as indoors?

- Are you willing to serve four years of apprenticeship in the sheet-metal industry?
- Are you willing to get your hands dirty?
- Would you like to be a skilled union sheet-metal worker?

It is not necessary to answer yes to all these questions, but anyone with seven or more positive responses should have good prospects for success in this field, according to the Training Fund. Of course, questions about apprenticeships and union membership may not apply in a nonunion setting, but the other questions should have applicability in most areas of the sheet-metal field. If you consider them carefully and can answer in the affirmative to most of them, a sheet-metal career may be worth exploring further.

4

MACHINING AND
MACHINE OPERATION

ONE OF THE most important areas of the metalworking industry is machining. This involves the production of metal parts, many of them small and precise, for various uses. Machinists make or repair precision parts that must be produced individually or in small quantities, rather than through an assembly line or other automated process. Machine operators, on the other hand, perform related work but on a different scale. They operate machines that produce equipment parts or other devices, often in large quantities.

Both types of jobs offer a wide range of opportunities. Because their work is so basic to any manufacturing process, persons with the right skills in this area are often in great demand in a variety of industries.

Work Performed by Machinists

Machinists produce various items made of iron, steel, brass, aluminum, and other metals. In most cases, these items must conform to specifications provided to them with each particular task assigned. For example, a machinist may build a component of a printing press, airplane engine, industrial machine, or other piece of equipment. This may involve developing a new part from scratch or duplicating one that has become worn out or broken.

In producing such items, machinists may perform tasks such as the following:

- Reading blueprints or other written specifications
- Taking precise measurements
- Selecting appropriate metal stock
- Planning steps for completing a job, from cutting the initial shape to finishing or polishing the surface
- Making mathematical calculations by hand or with a calculator
- Operating equipment such as drills, grinders, and lathes
- Using various types of equipment to cut, drill, or otherwise shape items being manufactured or modified
- Operating automated equipment such as numerical control equipment
- Writing or adapting computer programs for numerical control equipment
- Finishing and assembling machined components
- Testing and adjusting parts that have been manufactured

Because of the precise nature of their work, machinists typically work slowly and methodically. They often earn a great deal of respect from other workers because their work is seen as highly skilled and crucial to the manufacturing process. A commitment to high quality is often a major mode of operation in the machine shop setting.

An especially interesting aspect of machinists' work is that it is becoming increasingly automated. Computer-controlled equipment has allowed machinists to become more productive than ever and has added a fascinating element to this career area.

Roles of Machine Operators

Although related to machinists, machine operators generally represent a separate category of workers. A major difference is that they tend to concentrate on high-volume production rather than the small quantities dealt with by machinists.

The U.S. Department of Labor has provided the following description of the work of a machine operator, emphasizing the fabrication process.

> Sets up and operates machine tools, such as lathes, milling machines, boring machines, and grinders, to machine metallic and nonmetallic work pieces according to specifications, tooling instructions, and standard charts, applying knowledge of machining methods. Reads blueprint or job order for product specifications, such as dimensions and tolerances, and tooling instructions, such as fixtures, feed rates, cutting speeds, depth of cut, and determines sequence of operations. Selects, positions, and secures tool in tool-holder (chuck, collet, or toolpost). Positions and secures work piece in holding device, machine table, chuck, centers, or fixtures, using clamps and wrenches. Moves controls to position tool and work-piece in relation to each other and to set specified feeds, speeds, and depth of cut. Sets up fixture or feeding device, starts machine, and turns handwheel to feed tool to work piece or

vice versa, and engages feed. Turns valve handle to direct flow of coolant or cutting oil against tool and work piece. Observes operation of machine and verifies conformance of machined work piece to specifications, using measuring instruments, such as fixed gauges, calipers, and micrometers. Operates bench grinder to sharpen tools. May set up and operate machines and equipment other than machine tools, such as welding machines and flame-cutting equipment.

With the increased use of plastics in manufacturing, this area of metalworking also may include working with plastics. Some people employed in the field work with both metal and plastic, while others work only with one of the two materials.

A major employer in this field is the automotive industry. Many workers are needed to produce the large quantities of parts needed in the production of motor vehicles. Large numbers of workers also are employed in the mass production of fabricated metal products, primary metal products, electrical and electronic equipment, and machinery.

Machine operators often specialize in running one or two types of equipment. For example, workers may operate a machine that produces ball bearings or coats a metal machine component with another type of metal. Their responsibilities may include feeding materials through the equipment, monitoring factors such as volume and temperature, and observing safety standards necessary in using automated equipment.

Related Job Titles

According to the U.S. Department of Labor, job titles held by those working in machining and related areas include the following:

Carbide-die maker
Diamond-die maker
Die barber
Die designer
Die finisher
Drill-press operator
Drill sharpener
Engine lathe operator, numerical control
Gear-cutting-machine operator
Grinder, gear
Grinder, machine
Machine set-up operator
Machinist
Machinist apprentice
Machinist, experimental
Milling machine operator
Mold stamper
Numerical-control-machine operator
Reamer operator
Screw-machine operator
Surface-grinding-machine operator
Template maker, extrusion die
Tool-and-die maker
Tool repairer
Valve grinder

Working Conditions

Unlike some other related fields, machining and machine operations seldom involve outdoor work. Instead, most work is performed in shops or factories. This means that the daily working environment will not provide a great deal of variety, but workers are spared the discomfort of adapting to weather conditions.

Machinists may work in a small shop setting or in a larger factory. Good lighting and ventilation are the norm.

Machine operators often work on assembly lines in large factories. Such settings may be noisy, poorly lit, and crowded. This is not always the case, however, especially in more modern facilities.

In both types of jobs, workers may need to wear special safety equipment, such as goggles, earplugs, or protective shoes. They may also need to avoid wearing loose-fitting clothing or jewelry that could become caught in machinery.

Getting Trained

Persons who want to learn machining or machine operations can choose from several types of training. In some cases, this can be obtained on the job when an employer is willing to hire an untrained person and allow the individual to learn from other workers while conducting actual work for the company. This is the norm in machine operations, which in most settings is considered a less advanced skill than machining itself. Sometimes on-the-job training is also possible in machining. For machinists, entry into the field is usually based on completing a formal training program. This may be an apprenticeship program, not unlike that followed by sheetmetal workers but focusing on different skills. Or it might mean attending a vocational school, trade school, or two-year college. Chapter 8 covers these options in more detail.

Some of the more advanced machining skills can be learned in community, junior, or technical colleges. Many colleges across

North America offer programs in this area. Men and women who enroll in such programs study a comprehensive array of techniques and background information. For example, a typical program of this type is offered by Central Piedmont Community College (CPCC) in Charlotte, North Carolina. Students may earn a machinist diploma by completing a typical program of courses, in the case of CPCC, including the following:

- Machine Technology I, II, III, and IV
- Introduction to Computer Numerical Control Programming
- CNC Turning
- Advanced CNC Turning
- Blueprint Reading/Machining I and II
- Introduction to Metrology
- Machining Calculations
- Advanced Machining Calculations
- Advanced CNC Turning
- CNC Milling
- Introduction to Metallurgy

After successfully completing these and related courses, including a course in applied communications, students earn a diploma that qualifies them for jobs in the industry.

As an example of a program that emphasizes recent trends in the use of advanced technologies, Iowa's Kirkwood Community College offers an associate degree program in computer numerical control (CNC) machining. This program takes two years (equaling four semesters and one summer) of full-time study. Students learn to program, edit, set up, and operate CNC lathes and mills that are controlled by computers. They also learn quality control methods, such as statistical process control, the use of special quality control equipment, and advanced automated production methods.

Other examples include the machining technology programs offered by Randolph Community College in Asheboro, North Carolina, where students may earn an associate degree (with thirteen courses in the major area), diploma (seven courses), or certificate (six courses). Students learn about the theory and safe use of hand tools, power machinery, computerized equipment, and precision inspection instruments. The courses also cover topics such as learning to interpret blueprints, setting up manual and computer-controlled machines, performing basic and advanced machining operations, and making decisions to ensure that work quality is maintained.

Graduates qualify for jobs as machining technicians in manufacturing industries, public institutions, government agencies, and specialty machining and tool-and-die job shops.

In each program, students learn about machining operations related to metalworking industries. Topics covered include machine shop safety, measuring tools, lathes, drilling machines, saws, milling machines, bench grinders, surface grinding, and layout instruments. Students also study blueprint reading and machining calculations from basic calculations to practical machine shop applications and problems.

Degree and diploma students study advanced and special machining operations, CNC turning, CNC milling, the principles and applications of die making, the application and use of jigs and fixtures, the principles of mold making, and advanced applications and practical experience in the manufacturing of complex parts. They also complete general courses in areas such as social or behavioral sciences, humanities, fine arts, English, and math.

Typical courses completed by associate degree students include the following:

- Blueprint Reading
- Expository Writing
- Machining Technology I
- CNC Turning
- Machining Calculations
- Blueprint Reading: Mechanical
- Professional Research and Reporting
- Machining Technology II
- CNC Milling
- Advanced Machining Calculations
- Machining Technology III
- Introduction to CAD/CAM
- Cooperative Work Experience I
- Machining Technology IV
- Advanced CNC Milling
- Die Making I
- Geometry and Trigonometry
- Advanced CNC Turning
- Jig and Fixtures I
- Mold Construction I
- Humanities/Fine Arts Course
- Social/Behavioral Science Course
- Computer-Aided Manufacturing I

To complete an associate degree, students normally complete 70 to 72 credit hours. A certificate may be earned after completing 12 to 18 hours, and a diploma with 37 to 38 credit hours.

For another example of the diverse options available, Fullerton College in Fullerton, California, allows students to pursue any of six certificates in the machine tools area. In addition, an associate degree program in manufacturing technology is available with machining as an optional area of specialization.

Course offerings include the following:

- CNC Machine Set Up and Operation
- Advanced CNC Set Up and Operation
- Introduction to Machine Tools
- Intermediate Machine Tools
- Advanced Machine Tools
- CNC Parts Programming
- Blueprint Reading for the Metal Trades
- Geometric Dimensioning and Tolerancing
- Technical Mathematics
- Fundamentals of Drafting
- Wire EDM: Programming and Operation
- Fundamentals of Metallurgy
- Manufacturing Processes
- Industrial Safety
- Introduction to Welding
- AutoCAD for Industry
- Advanced CNC Programming Using SURFCAM
- Intermediate Machine Tools
- Technical Science

As an example of options available to advanced students, Conestoga College in Guelph, Ontario, offers a postgraduate program in computer numerical control machining. The program allows those with a background in metal machining to acquire a working knowledge of computer numerical machines. This includes an understanding of the principles of numerical control, its application to metal cutting machine tools, and writing CNC programs.

Students develop a working knowledge of CNC machine tool consoles, safe activation of their modes of operation, and safe working practices.

Course offerings include the following.

- Principles of Computerized Numerical Control
- Fundamentals of Manual Program
- Computerized Numerical Control Machine Tool Consoles
- Computerized Numerical Control Set-Up and Operating Procedures

One of the most helpful features of many schools is that they maintain close ties with local industries. Typically, this includes regular meetings between faculty and members of an advisory committee made up of machinists, supervisors, owners of small shops, and managers in larger manufacturing firms. They not only help make certain the college teaches its students the right skills but also often strengthen chances for graduates to land good jobs after completing their training.

Many Options

As can be seen from the examples offered here, career options in machining and machine operation are quite diverse.

5

STRUCTURAL AND
REINFORCING METALWORKING

STRUCTURAL AND REINFORCING metal workers perform important work. These workers, also known as ironworkers, play a central role in the construction industry by erecting the framework around which other parts of structures are built. Ironworkers build the steel frameworks of large buildings. They perform similar functions in the construction of bridges. They also provide reinforcing for concrete structures, install metal components of buildings such as steel stairs and walls, work with equipment for hoisting and lifting metal, and perform related work.

A simple way to view the role of ironworkers is to compare their efforts with those performed by sheet-metal workers as discussed previously. Whereas sheet-metal workers tend to deal with the outer "skin" of structures, structural and reinforcing metal workers concentrate more on their "skeletons." Just as the skeleton of a human body supports the rest of its anatomy, the metal beams, rods, bars, and other parts assembled by ironworkers form the internal framework for buildings and other structures. The U.S. Department of Labor has provided this job description for an ironworker.

> Performs any combination of following duties to raise, place, and unite girders, columns, and other structural-steel members to form completed structures or structure frameworks, working as member of crew. Sets up hoisting equipment for raising and placing structural-steel members. Fastens steel members to cable of hoist, using chain, cable, or rope. Signals worker operating hoisting equipment to lift and place steel member. Guides member, using tab line (rope) or rides on member in order to guide it into position. Pulls, pushes, or pries steel members into approximate position while member is supported by hoisting device. Forces members into final position, using turnbuckles, crowbars, jacks, and handtools. Aligns rivet holes in member with corresponding holes in previously placed member by driving drift pins or handle of wrench through holes. Verifies vertical and horizontal alignment of members, using plumb bob and level. Bolts aligned members to keep them into position until they can be permanently riveted, bolted, or welded in place. Catches hot rivets tossed by rivet heater (heat treating) in bucket and inserts rivets in holes, using tongs. Bucks (holds) rivets while river, pneumatic (any industry) uses air hammer to form heads on rivets. Cuts and welds steel members to make alterations, using oxyacetylene welding equipment.

Typical Duties

Typical duties performed by ironworkers may include the following:

- Setting up cranes and derricks used to lift building materials high into the air for construction of a multistory office building

- Unloading steel beams from a truck and stacking them for later use in building a bridge
- Attaching a cable from a crane to a steel girder so it can be hoisted into position
- Reading blueprints in preparation for building a steel water tower
- Using bolts and hand tools to connect beams that will support the walls of a new warehouse
- Joining steel rods together to help form the roof for a new building
- Positioning rods to form reinforcing for a floor that will be made of concrete
- Installing a metal fire escape on the outside of a large apartment building
- Assembling a storage tank for heating oil at a factory
- Putting together the metal portions of a steel-and-concrete bridge
- Setting steel bars in place to reinforce concrete
- Cutting and fitting wire mesh for concrete reinforcement
- Using hand signals to direct hoist operators
- Assisting in hoisting beams or other materials above the ground
- Operating laser alignment equipment
- Repairing metal structures
- Installing metal window frames
- Installing metal stairways
- Assembling ornamental enhancements to buildings
- Erecting industrial storage tanks

As with other metalworking fields, much variety may be found from one type of job to the next. Many ironworkers, however, specialize in one type of work. For example, one person may work mostly in the construction of large buildings. Another may specialize in ornamental metalwork. Still another may work primarily in road and bridge construction.

Most ironworkers are employed by large construction companies. Unlike machining or sheet-metal work, relatively few small businesses exist in this field due to the large amounts of money required for equipment as well as materials such as steel beams.

The majority of jobs are usually found in large and medium-sized cities. Some ironworkers either relocate to find work or they are sent long distances by their employers, but this is not necessarily a requirement.

Related Job Titles

Related job titles include the following.

Coil winder
Electrical and electronic equipment assembler
Electromechanical equipment assembler
Engine assembler
Fiberglass laminator and fabricator
Finisher
Ornamental ironworker
Reinforcing iron and rebar worker
Structural metal fabricator and fitter
Systems assembler
Taper
Team assembler
Timing device assembler

Working Conditions

By the very nature of their jobs, most structural and reinforcing metalworkers must spend a great deal of time outdoors. Often, the part of the structure they are building must be completed before walls or roofs are installed, thus exposing workers to the vagaries of weather conditions. These can vary according to location and season. Hot summer days can impose an unavoidable degree of discomfort, as can wind and rain. In many parts of North America, workers also must face cold weather for at least part of the year, including snow, sleet, and subfreezing temperatures. Such conditions not only affect individual comfort but also restrict working schedules. Bad weather can delay completion of projects and result in lost working days.

Working conditions for ironworkers often involve the additional factor of height. Many jobs in this field require working high above the ground. The most graphic example of this element of the job might be the construction of a huge office building in a large city. In such a setting, a worker might be perched sixty stories or more above the ground, walking across narrow beams. But even working a few feet above the ground poses special safety requirements as well as the mental or psychological ability to cope with such settings.

Right Skills

The skills necessary for working as an ironworker can be acquired by both men and women who have the necessary basic traits upon which to build.

First among these traits are basic manual skills. Ironworkers must use tools and apply a basic understanding of mechanical principles;

thus you should have an aptitude for such things, even if you have not learned a great deal about the details of using various tools. Do you enjoy working with your hands? Do you have a good eye for detail? Does the idea of working as an ironworker seem to match the way you see yourself in the world of work? A positive answer to these questions would help for a career in this field to become a reality.

Another basic trait needed is physical fitness. Working in this field often involves hard, physical labor. You must be physically fit to succeed. This does not mean you must have bulging muscles or be a large person; after all, the really heavy lifting may be handled by machines. But at the same time, some degree of strength is needed. Agility, stamina, and the ability to work at substantial heights above the ground, if necessary, also will be assets.

Anyone who works in this field should also be highly conscious of safety or at least have the capacity for developing such a trait. Constant attention to this factor is needed to avoid falls or other accidents.

Getting Trained

Most ironworkers acquire their skills on the job or through an apprenticeship. A high school diploma may be needed, but it is not necessary to attend college to break into this field.

If you seek a position in which the employer will provide on-the-job training, your case will be strengthened if you have taken vocational courses in high school. Or, if you can demonstrate an aptitude for working with tools and a willingness to learn, you may have an edge over other applicants.

Probably the best way to pursue a career as an ironworker is to complete a formal apprenticeship. Such opportunities are provided by the International Association of Bridge, Structural, and Ornamental Ironworkers in cooperation with contractors who employ workers. Completion of an apprenticeship requires three years of on-the-job training plus at least 144 hours of classroom study each year.

Subjects studied during an apprenticeship include the following.

- Use of tools
- Material properties and handling
- Basic math applications
- Safety procedures
- Structural erecting
- Rigging
- Welding
- Ornamental assembling

In addition to these subjects, apprentices gain experience on the job in the various tasks expected of full-fledged workers. Generally, they develop greater independence as time passes, and their skill levels grow. Additional information about training options is provided in Chapter 8.

6

Welding

Welding may be the most well-known type of metalworking. In welding, workers join two or more pieces of metal (or sometimes other materials) through use of heat, pressure, or a related process. The result is that the metals become fused together.

Welders help build automobiles, ships, airplanes, buildings, bridges, appliances, and many other items made in whole or in part of metal. They also may repair metallic items. To do such work, welders use special equipment and apply job-specific knowledge. Because their work is needed in a variety of industries, men and women who can perform welding functions continue to enjoy demand for their services throughout the United States and Canada.

Types of Welding

Although it has existed for more than a century, welding is a field that keeps changing with new technological developments. Welding was first developed in the 1880s in Europe and America. Over the years, experts in the field have developed a wide range of welding processes. Today's welding techniques include the following:

- **Gas welding.** This is one of the most basic types of welding. A special torch is used to burn acetylene or another flammable gas, which produces a flame hot enough to melt metal. In its basic form, gas welding involves the use of a handheld torch operated by a single person.
- **Arc welding.** In this welding process, high temperatures are generated by an electric arc instead of burning gases. In most cases, a generator is employed to produce electric current, which is then used to create the arc that jumps between the metal surface and the welder's tool—either an electrode or a welding rod. Arc welding can be a simple, one-person task or a complex, automated process.
- **Resistance welding.** This process is different from arc welding in that instead of an arc, the flow of electricity between two pieces of metal creates resistance, and they become fused together.
- **Advanced technologies.** Other types of welding are based on recent high-tech advancements. For example, some advanced types of welding involve the use of sound waves, lasers, or electron beams.

Multiple Roles

Welders work in many major industries. They help assemble some of the largest and most important structures in the civilized world.

Building Construction

Many welders work in the building construction industry. This is especially common in erecting large buildings of steel and concrete.

For a multistory office building, for example, welders connect beams, steel reinforcing rods, and other parts of the steel super-structure. They perform similar work in building other structures, such as sports stadiums, manufacturing facilities, instructional buildings at schools and colleges, and warehouses. For buildings made of all types of materials, metal beams and other elements of the basic support structure must be welded.

Because welding is such an important facet of the construction industry, job openings for welders can occur in all kinds of settings across the United States and Canada. This includes large cities, sub-urban areas, and small towns. Some jobs, such as assembling components for prefabricated buildings, involve staying in one location and working in a shop environment. Others require traveling from one construction site to the next.

Road and Bridge Construction

Another major area of employment for welders is road and bridge construction. Welders help build guard rails, steel reinforcing por-tions of concrete highways, and bridges—including large bridges for major highways and small bridges for less-traveled roads. In addition to building new bridges, such work often involves repair-ing existing structures.

Automobile Industry

Thousands of welders are employed in the automobile industry. They play an important part in assembling the millions of cars and trucks produced every year. For example, a welder in this industry may specialize in operating an automated welding machine as part of a car assembly line. Or a welder might work in the auto repair industry instead of manufacturing. Such work might involve welding damaged exhaust pipes, radiators, or auto body parts. In fact, many people first master welding skills to perform this kind of work and then expand their skills into other welding areas.

Shipbuilding

Still another major area in which welding plays a key role is shipbuilding. Although ships are produced in much smaller quantities than cars, that factor may be offset by the tremendous size of many ships. Building just one ship can keep a large crew of workers busy for many months.

The work involved in shipbuilding can be quite rewarding. The end product may be an aircraft carrier, submarine, cargo ship, or supertanker. Helping construct such a huge structure can be an exciting process. And since such large amounts of metal must be used in building a single ship, the role played by welders is extremely important.

Aircraft Construction

Welders perform equally vital work in aircraft construction. They help construct huge jets and other commercial aircraft, small airplanes, helicopters, and a variety of military aircraft. Welders in this industry must meet special standards of performance due to safety regulations. They must work with great care and produce results that are free of errors. As with construction of ships, workers can experience special feelings of satisfaction when they see the end result of their efforts. For many people, the sense of accomplishment in building sophisticated flying machines can be substantial.

Tasks Performed

In these and other industries, the specific job tasks performed by welders include a variety of functions. Typical work completed by men and women in such roles might include the following:

- Operating a welding machine in an auto assembly plant
- Welding pipes in a new shopping mall
- Repairing broken pipes in a manufacturing plant
- Assembling the fuselage of a jumbo jet
- Welding a boiler on a new cruise ship
- Connecting steel bars that will reinforce the concrete structure of a bridge
- Welding components of a multistory distillation system at an oil refinery
- Joining together sections of equipment in a factory that makes farm equipment
- Performing nontechnical functions such as buying welding supplies, attending safety classes, or filling out production reports

Related Job Titles

Welding is a diverse field. Following are just some of the job titles related to welding listed by the U.S. Department of Labor:

Acetylene welder
Apprentice arc welder
Arc cutter
Arc welder

Arc welder-fitter
Arc welding-machine operator
Brazer crawler
Brazer-machine feeder
Brazing-furnace feeder
Brazing-machine operator
Burning-machine operator
Certified welder gas cutter
Combination welder
Combination welder apprentice
Cylinder heads repairer
Electro-gas welding-machine operator
Electron-beam machine welder
Electron beam welding-machine operator
Electronic brazer
Electronic-eye-thermal-cutting-machine operator
Electronic solderer
Electroslag welding-machine operator
Experimental welder
Explosion welder
Flame-brazing-machine operator
Flame-cutting-machine operator
Flame-cutting-machine-operator helper
Flame gouger
Flame planer
Flame scarfer
Flash brusher gas-cutting-machine operator
Flash-welding-machine operator
Flux-cored arc welder
Friction welding-machine operator

Furnace brazer
Furnace brazer helper
Furnace solderer
Gas-metal arc welder
Gas-metal arc welding-machine operator
Gas-tungsten arc cutter
Gas-tungsten arc welder
Gas-tungsten arc welding-machine operator
Gas welder
Gas welder apprentice
Gas welder-fitter
Gas welding-machine operator
Hand burner
Hand thermal cutter
Hydrogen braze-furnace operator
Induction brazer
Induction brazer helper
Induction-heating-equipment setter
Induction solderer
Laser-beam cutter
Laser-beam-machine operator
Lead burner
Lead-burner apprentice
Lead-burner supervisor
Machine feeder
Machine helper
Magnetic-thermal-cutting-machine operator
Oxyacetylene welder
Oxyhydrogen welder
Percussion-welding-machine operator

Performance-test inspector
Plasma arc cutter
Plasma arc welder
Plasma-cutting-machine operator
Production line brazer
Production line solderer
Production line welder
Production-welding-machine operator
Repair and salvage brazer
Resistance brazer
Setter resistance machine welder
Setter shielded-metal arc welder
Silver solderer
Solderer-assembler
Solderer-dipper
Soldering-machine feeder
Soldering-machine operator
Soldering-machine operator helper
Structural repair welder
Submerged arc hand welder
Submerged arc welding-machine operator
Tack welder
Thermal-cutter helper
Thermal-cutting-tracer-machine operator
Thermit welding-machine operator
Tool-and-die welder
Torch brazer
Torch cutter
Torch solderer
Ultrasonic welding-machine operator

Upset-welding-machine operator
Weld inspector
Welder-fitter
Welder-fitter apprentice
Welder helper
Welding equipment repairer
Welding-machine feeder
Welding-machine-operator helper
Welding-machine tender
Welding tester

What It Takes

Anyone interested in a welding career should have certain basic aptitudes and the ability to master additional skills. For most workers,
these qualities will include most or all of the following.

- Good manual skills (ability to use tools, adequate hand-to-
  eye coordination)
- Attention to detail
- Patience
- Dependability
- Pride in doing a good job
- Awareness of safety considerations
- Dexterity
- Physical stamina
- Good eyesight (or eyesight that can be corrected with
  contact lenses or glasses)
- A steady hand
- Curiosity and willingness to learn

Of course, individual traits vary, and you can compensate for some weaknesses with hard work or creative approaches. For instance, if you are not particularly dexterous, that ability can be improved with exercises or repetition of basic tasks. If you have not had enough experience with hand tools to know whether you can use them effectively, taking a shop class or experimenting on your own can give some indications of your potential. The main point is to be realistic about your abilities and aptitudes. Then you can compare them to the requirements of a welding career and decide what you need to do to compete in the field.

Working Conditions

Working conditions for welders vary. They may work outdoors in various types of weather or indoors in a more controlled environment. Sometimes the job may involve operating in a confined area designed to contain glare and sparks. Outdoors, welders may work on scaffolds or platforms at substantial heights off the ground. Indoors or out, the work may require lifting heavy objects or maintaining a variety of awkward positions while bending, stooping, or standing.

Getting Trained

You probably will need to complete some type of training program to become a welder. Most people acquire welding capabilities through one or more of these training options:

- Industry-sponsored training programs
- Government-sponsored training programs
- Apprenticeships

- High school vocational programs
- Trade and technical schools
- Community and junior colleges
- Technical colleges
- Military training programs

Descriptions of two typical welding programs are included here. The first is the North Island College in Courtenay, British Columbia. It offers programs in welding that prepare students to work in various industries and to take welder performance qualification testing. These include three options taking from two to twelve months to complete.

The Provincial C Level Welding program is self-paced. Students use a combination of audiovisual and printed resources, up-to-date shop facilities, and instruction from qualified instructors. For a student attending on a full-time basis, completion time is normally six to eight months. After graduating from this program, the student must gain appropriate work experience before receiving registration as a C Level welder. The total of training time and work experience time must reach at least twelve months.

During the training period, students complete the following modules or courses:

- Introduction to Welding
- Oxy-Fuel Cutting
- Gas Welding and Braze Welding
- Shielded Metal Arc Welding
- Air Carbon Arc Cutting and Plasma Arc Cutting
- Basic Gas Metal and Flux Core Arc Welding
- Rigging and Material Handling
- Metallurgy I

The Level B program can be completed in about four months of full-time training, followed by eight months of industrial work experience. The Level A program consists of approximately two months of training and ten months of work experience.

The second is Shasta College in Redding, California. It offers a program in welding technology that leads to an associate of science degree. Students complete 60 units of instruction including major course work (39.5 units) and additional general education (13 units) as well as electives (5.5 units). For those who wish to complete a shorter program, a certificate can be earned after completion of 34.5 units.

Courses offered include the following:

- **Welding.** This course in general welding includes both oxyacetylene and arc welding. Students learn about repair welding, welding symbols, trade terminology, care and use of various types of welding equipment, and safety procedures.
- **Beginning Welding.** This beginning course covers basic welding skills to be used in a trade or service occupation. Emphasis is placed on oxyacetylene and arc welding in all positions.
- **General Welding/Shop Metals.** This course covers the fundamentals of metalworking. Topics addressed include metal identification, proper and safe use of hand tools, power tools, bench metals, welding, and machine-tool operations.
- **Introduction to Arc Welding.** This course includes power sources; electrode identification; weldability of metals; joint design, air arc, and oxyacetylene cutting; and introduction to GTAW (gas tungsten arc welding) and GMAW (gas metal arc welding). Students learn to weld stringer and weave beads, and butt and fillet welds in flat, horizontal, vertical, and overhead positions.

- **Intermediate Arc Welding.** This course emphasizes vertical and overhead welding and prepares students for weld certification and advanced arc welding classes. Covers weld symbols and aluminum arc and cast iron welding.
- **Sheet Metal Fabrication (Residential and Commercial).** This is an introductory-level course on residential and commercial sheet-metal working. It includes classroom and laboratory instruction in sheet-metal equipment, parallel and transition layout and duct construction, duct installations, residential and commercial duct systems and materials as related to heating and cooling systems, and flashings and flashing installations.
- **Structural Steel Metal Fabrication.** This is an introductory course in metal fabrication, blueprint reading and sketching, including layout, production welding, and the use of metal fabrication equipment.
- **Structural Steel GMAW and FCAW (Flux Core Arc Welding).** This course covers GMAW with structural steel while stressing certification code welding on plate and structural steel in all positions. Topics addressed include gas metal and flux core arc welding equipment and welding variables, shielding gases, troubleshooting equipment and weld defects, welder certification and welding codes, weld symbols, structural steel identification and welding procedures, and metallurgy.
- **TIG Welding.** This course on TIG (Tungsten Inert Gas) welding (also known as Heliarc) covers aluminum, mild steel, stainless steel, magnesium, and copper welding. Metals identification and weld symbols are included.
- **GMAW MIG Welding (Light Gauge and Nonferrous Metal).** This course emphasizes development of MIG (Metallic Inert Gas) welding skills on light gauge steel, stainless steel, and alu-

minum. Related instruction includes ferrous and nonferrous metal identification and their welding characteristics, MIG welding applications and variables, inert shielding gases and mixtures, troubleshooting MIG equipment and welds, and spot welding.

• **Pipe Welding Fundamentals.** This course covers pipe welding with an emphasis on open groove pipe joints using oxyacetylene, arc, and inert gas welding processes in all positions.

• **Advanced Arc Welding.** This advanced course prepares students to pass structural steel certification in vertical and overhead positions.

• **Advanced GTAW (TIG) Welding.** This advanced laboratory class has an emphasis on vertical and overhead welding. The thrust is on helping students improve their beginning skills to prepare them for entry into the job force as a TIG welder.

• **Advanced Pipe Welding.** This advanced pipe welding class has an emphasis on ASME, AWS, or API certification. It covers welding codes and pipe classification and identification.

• **Advanced GMAW (MIG) Welding.** This is an advanced welding lab class with emphasis on vertical and overhead welding. It is designed for students interested in improving their beginning skills to prepare them for entry into the job force as a GMAW (MIG) welder.

• **Special Topics in Welding Technology.** This course gives students an opportunity to explore a variety of topics dealing with changing knowledge in the field of welding technology.

Other schools offer similar programs, although details such as the length of the program and the courses offered vary. For more details about a given school or program, access the school's website or review a copy of its course catalog.

More details on educational alternatives are provided in Chapter 8. Whichever option you choose, it is important to realize that a short-term investment of your time can pay off for many years to come. Most welding programs take only weeks or months to complete, meaning that even if you do not enjoy going to school, the commitment on your part will be manageable. Anyone with motivation and the qualities described in this chapter should be able to complete one of these training programs successfully.

7

JEWELRY MAKING

IN CONSIDERING METALWORKING, the first image that comes to mind will probably be of a bridge, building, appliance, or some other relatively large structure or object. But the range of metalworking careers includes not just industrial applications but also fine, detailed work. One career area of this type is working as a jeweler or jewelry repairer.

Jewelers and related workers make or repair various kinds of jewelry including necklaces, bracelets, rings, earrings, pins, and other forms of adornment. In the process, they may complete work that is quite detailed and very precise.

What Jewelers Do

Work that jewelers typically perform might include any of the following activities:

• Setting precious and semiprecious stones in engagement rings and other rings while working in a small manufacturing plant

• Repairing broken jewelry in a repair shop, where an ordinary day's work might include fixing broken clasps of necklaces and bracelets, adjusting the sizes of rings, or replacing jewels in rings or other items

• Managing a small retail store where duties combine repairing jewelry, supervising employees, and managing the overall business operations

• Making jewelry from designs produced by others or designing new pieces and then assembling them

Following is a general job description developed by the U.S. Department of Labor for the positions of jeweler, jewelry jobber, and jewelry repairer.

> Fabricates and repairs jewelry articles, such as rings, brooches, pendants, bracelets, and lockets. Forms model of article from wax or metal, using carving tools. Places wax model in casting ring and pours plaster into ring to form mold. Inserts plaster mold in furnace to melt wax. Casts metal model from plaster mold. Forms mold of sand or rubber from metal model for casting jewelry. Pours molten metal into mold or operates centrifugal casting machine to cast article . . . Cuts, saws, files, and polishes article, using hand tools and polishing wheel. Solders pieces of jewelry together, using soldering torch or iron. Enlarges or reduces size of rings by sawing through band, adding or removing metal, and soldering ends together. Repairs broken clasps, pins, rings, and other jewelry by soldering or replacing broken parts. Reshapes and restyles old jewelry, following designs or instructions, using hand tools and machines, such as jeweler's lathe and drill. Smoothes soldered joints and rough spots using hand file and emery paper.

May be designated according to metals fashioned as Goldsmith (jewelry-silver); as Platinumsmith (jewelry-silver); or as Silver-smith (jewelry-silver).

The type of work setting varies widely. Persons employed in the manufacturing of jewelry may work in a large shop or factory, while those employed at the retail level may work in a large department store or a small jewelry store. In a retail setting, the job may include interacting with customers in addition to the hands-on work performed. In some situations, jewelers or jewelry repairers may operate their own small businesses.

Creative Angle

One of the most interesting aspects of the jewelry-making field is the potential for creativity. While in some cases the work may consist of duplicating designs in accordance with specific instructions provided by a supervisor, in others the jeweler may develop his or her own designs. For example, a jeweler in a small shop may create a brooch or pendant without consulting a design or model, or he or she may fashion a piece of jewelry based on the special request of a customer. This can add an element of artistic creativity that greatly enhances the enjoyment of job performance.

Another important feature of the work of jewelers is the need to be conscious of security. By its very nature, jewelry is often extremely valuable. Items made of precious metals such as gold or silver may be worth hundreds or thousands of dollars, and this value can be increased even more when gems such as diamonds, rubies, sapphires, or emeralds are added. As a result, working with jewelry can include significant financial responsibilities.

Jewelers and related workers must not only be honest themselves, but they must also guard against possible dishonesty by others. Their job duties may include the following:

- Maintaining an accurate, up-to-date inventory of jewelry and working materials
- Storing jewelry and components in locked storage areas and making certain they are secured when not being used
- Operating electronic alarms and other advanced security systems
- Treating working materials with great care to avoid damage or loss

Related Job Titles

The U.S. Department of Labor has listed dozens of job titles for work in the jewelry industry. Some examples are as follows:

Annealer
Assembler
Bracelet and brooch maker
Bracelet maker, novelty
Caster
Caster helper
Chain-maker, hand
Chain-maker, machine
Chain mender
Die cutter
Die maker

Driller
Earring maker
Engraving supervisor
Goldsmith
Jewelry-engraving supervisor
Jigsawyer
Lathe hand
Lathe operator
Link assembler
Linker
Locket maker
Melter
Mesh cutter
Molder, bench
Platinumsmith
Ring maker
Ring stamper
Rolled-gold plater
Roller
Sample maker
Scraper
Scratch brusher
Silversmith
Solderer
Stringer-up, soldering machine
Supervisor, jewelry department
Trophy assembler
Watchband assembler
Wire drawer

Career Pluses

Each career area has its own particular advantages, but those of the jewelry-making field set it apart in some ways from other metalworking careers. Some of these advantageous factors are as follows:

• **Comfortable working conditions.** Unlike many other persons who work with metal, jewelers and related workers often work in comfortable, attractive, indoor settings. These may range from a shop environment to a retail store.

• **Limited physical requirements.** Although good eyesight and the ability to work well with one's hands are necessary, there is no need for physical strength, climbing ability, or other such physically demanding job traits. Thus persons who may not feel suited to the rigors of a career as an ironworker, for instance, may find jewelry making a more appropriate metalworking field.

• **Potential links with other careers.** Men and women who start out in this field may find that it leads to other career areas. For example, some jewelry-making jobs might lead to supervisory positions in retail stores, sales positions, or other related work.

Getting Trained

Jewelers and related workers usually acquire their skills through on-the-job training or by attending a trade or technical school, or through a combination of these options. A high school diploma may be needed before pursuing one of these training approaches, but collegiate study is not necessary.

Students who attend trade or technical schools take classes covering such subjects as basic jewelry-making skills, repair techniques, use and care of tools and machines, casting, and polishing. They may also study math and blueprint reading. The length of programs varies from one school to the next, with some programs taking as few as six months to complete and others lasting two years or more.

As one example, North Bennet Street School in Boston, Massachusetts, offers a two-year program in jewelry making and repair. Students who complete this program acquire the fundamentals of jewelry fabrication and stone setting. Through completion of practical projects, students develop skills in the following:

- Working with tools of the trade
- Applying techniques of metal forming
- Polishing, soldering, engraving
- Fabricating silver and gold
- Working with metals and stones
- Making wax models
- Repairing jewelry
- Working at higher levels of jewelry making
- Setting stones

In addition, the program covers the essentials of repair techniques including resizing rings and repairing other types of jewelry. For more details, contact:

North Bennet Street School
39 North Bennet Street
Boston, Massachusetts 02113
www.nbss.org

Some manufacturers and other employers offer in-house training programs. Students learn skills similar to those in trade school programs but usually with special emphasis on the specific needs of the employer. For example, a company that provides engraving services may spend a substantial amount of training time on this skill, while another company that does not specialize in engraving may skip the subject entirely. A firm that produces a limited number of jewelry types may deal only with those particular products in its training activities.

In any case, some type of training usually is necessary to work in this field. More information on training opportunities is provided in Chapter 8, and schools that offer training for jewelers are listed in Appendix A.

8

TRAINING OPTIONS

WORKING WITH METAL requires special knowledge and skills. To pursue a career in this field, you will need to complete one or more of the following steps:

• **Learn informally on the job.** Some employers will hire inexperienced workers and then expect them to learn metalworking skills by observing other workers or having more experienced personnel teach them the basics. This is more common with nonunion employers and small companies than with large corporations. Such measures are in some ways less desirable than structured training programs because they do not cover as much detail. Also, informal training options are not always available, especially in some of the more complex metalworking fields.

• **Participate in a formal on-the-job training program.** This might consist of an apprenticeship sponsored by a company, a trade union, or both. Or it might be a short-term program offered by an employer. In either case, each participant will follow a structured approach, and completion of such a program normally will be required of all new employees.

• **Go to school.** For some metalworking fields, the best way to get started is to attend a school offering training in the appropriate area. This might be a vocational school, a trade or business school, or a two-year college. Which one depends upon the nature of the program and several other factors that will be discussed later in this chapter.

Whichever training approach you take, careful advance planning will help you avoid problems along the way. Be sure to ask yourself questions such as the following:

- What training options exist in the field in which I am interested?
- Are training programs in metalworking available in my geographical area?
- If training programs are not located nearby, am I willing to travel the necessary distance to participate in one?
- Am I willing to go on to more school after high school if need be?
- If I have a choice between attending a school or college and participating in on-the-job training, which choice will be best for me?
- Will I have to pay for training? If so, where will I obtain the funds?

In finding the answers to questions such as these, you will be taking the initial steps in preparing for a metalworking career.

Apprenticeships

In some metalworking fields, an effective way to learn the trade is to serve as an apprentice. This special learning format involves working under the supervision of one or more persons who have already had substantial job experience and are, therefore, qualified to help pass their knowledge on to newcomers.

Serving an apprenticeship is one of the oldest ways of learning a trade or craft. Since medieval times, workers have used this method of learning skilled trades. At one time, this was about the only way to master many trades, with basic techniques kept secret by practitioners and shared only with other workers in the field and apprentices.

In modern times, apprenticeships still play an important role in some areas, even though they are not as dominant as they once were. For persons who want to become sheet-metal workers, for instance, an apprenticeship is the preferred approach.

Sheet-Metal Apprenticeships

The Sheet Metal Workers International Association, a major union, requires its members to complete a structured apprenticeship. This training is offered through the International Training Institute for the Sheet Metal and Air Conditioning Industry. Persons who undergo such training must complete approximately eight thousand hours of supervised job experience and nearly six hundred hours of instruction over a period of about four years.

Some companies also provide apprenticeship training, usually in cooperation with a local union chapter.

A typical apprenticeship program might include the following:

Year One

Sign written agreements setting out program terms.

Begin working on the job.

Begin attending classes (which may meet one or more evenings per week, or may be held during the day).

Complete the probationary period (if required).

Learn basics of pattern layout and development.

Learn basics of drafting.

Practice use of hand tools.

Learn how to apply mathematics to the sheet-metal trade.

Master safety concepts and procedures.

Year Two

Continue working on the job.

Continue classroom training.

Emphasize increased knowledge of metals and their substitutes.

Develop skills in basic plan and specification reading.

Strengthen knowledge of triangulation, radial line, and parallel line development.

Year Three

Begin to work with less supervision from experienced workers.

Continue on-the-job training.

Continue classroom instruction.

Learn about solar installation.

Master soldering techniques.

Study hoisting and rigging.

Learn about energy management and retrofitting of environmental systems.

Year Four
Work with increasingly less supervision.
Read complex plans and specifications.
Increase knowledge of cooling, heating, and ventilation
    systems.
Master various welding techniques.
Understand functions of refrigeration components such as
    condensers and compressors.

At the end of the multiyear training period, the man or woman who successfully completes the program earns the title of *journeyman*. This means that the individual becomes a full-fledged worker in the field with equal status of other experienced workers. Employers and coworkers can count on the person's ability to complete a variety of tasks competently and efficiently.

Machining Apprenticeships

Similar options are offered in machining and other metalworking trades. For example, the International Association of Machinists and Aerospace Workers operates a basic apprenticeship program in cooperation with employers. The association has noted the following responsibilities of apprentices:

1. To diligently and faithfully perform the work of the trade and to perform such other pertinent duties as may be assigned by the employer's supervisor of apprentices, which are related to the apprentice's total training program

2. To not only respect the property of the employer but also abide by the rules and regulations of the employer, the union, and the committee

3. To regularly attend and satisfactorily complete the required hours of related instruction as required under this apprenticeship program

4. To maintain such records of work experience and training received on the job and in related instruction as may be required by the committee

5. To develop safe working habits and conduct themselves in their work in such a manner as to ensure their own safety and that of their fellow workers

6. To work for the employer to whom indentured by the completion of apprenticeship unless terminated by the committee. Not to seek employment with another employer within the jurisdictional area of this program without prior clearance of the committee, the union, and the employer to whom indentured

7. To conduct themselves, at all times, in a creditable, ethical, and moral manner, trying to realize that much time, money, and effort will be spent in affording the apprentice an opportunity to become a skilled journeyman

A Competency-Based Apprenticeship System

The National Institute for Metalworking Skills (NIMS) has recently developed an innovative competency-based apprenticeship system for the metalworking industry. This system was developed in partnership with the U.S. Department of Labor and with more than three hundred companies participating in its development. The resulting guidelines have been approved by the Department of Labor, and DOL apprenticeship staff at the national and state levels have been trained in the new system.

Areas covered by the new program include metal-forming (stamping, press brake, roll forming, laser cutting) and machining (machining, tool and die making, mold making, screw machining, machine building and machine maintenance, service and repair).

For more details, contact:

The National Institute for Metalworking Skills
10565 Fairfax Boulevard, Suite 203
Fairfax, Virginia 22030
www.nims-skills.org

Apprenticeship Pluses

The apprentice approach to training offers a number of advantages. It is not hurried or condensed, providing plenty of time to master the work involved. Participants benefit from direct, on-the-job experience and frequent contact with experienced workers. At the same time, they are earning a regular income that increases as they gain experience and knowledge.

On-the-Job Training

Employers who do not rely on the apprenticeship system may offer their own training for new employees. In larger companies, such training may consist of a formal class for a group of new workers. In other situations, one-on-one instruction may be provided. For example, a man who runs a small machine shop may hire an inexperienced person and then teach basic skills as the two work together in an informal learning format not greatly different from an apprenticeship.

How do you find out about company-sponsored training? Sometimes website postings, newspaper ads, or other announcements about job openings will indicate that new workers are needed and that training will be provided to successful applicants. In other cases, you may need to contact the personnel office at a company that employs workers in metalworking fields and ask if special training is offered.

In a small shop setting, it may be worthwhile to talk to the owner and ask what possibilities may exist for on-the-job training. For instance, a person who operates a small aluminum siding firm may be willing to teach the basics of the business to an inexperienced newcomer.

Government-Sponsored Training Programs

Another training alternative is provided by special training programs supported through funding from government agencies. Sometimes these programs are sponsored by employers, sometimes by schools or colleges, and sometimes by combinations of the two or by other agencies.

A prime example is training made possible through the Workforce Investment Act (WIA). This is a special initiative of the U.S. government to reduce unemployment and provide trained workers in a variety of fields. Under this program, organizations such as companies or schools receive extra funding to provide job-specific training or related services. To qualify for such training, you must meet certain eligibility requirements. To find out more, check with the local Workforce Investment Board (WIB) or the nearest branch of your state employment office.

Programs Offered by Schools and Colleges

In some metalworking fields, one of the best options available is to enroll in a trade school or two-year college that offers the appropriate training. For instance, classes in machining and welding are offered by many such institutions at both the trade school and collegiate levels. Programs for jewelers are offered by a number of schools, though not usually at the college level. On the other hand, sheet-metal work and ironwork usually are learned through some industry-sponsored training rather than schools.

Choosing the Right Type of School for You

If you are interested in a subject that is taught in trade or technical schools, it is important to take your time in selecting the school that will be best for you. This may sound simple, but you can make a major mistake by enrolling in a program without checking it out or considering similar programs offered by other schools. Each school has its own strengths and weaknesses, ranging from the quality of its instructional equipment to the kind of reputation it has with employers.

In taking a look at any school, it's important to realize exactly what kind of institution it is and how it compares with others. Is it a trade or technical school? A technical college? A junior or community college? The terms may sound similar, but there can be important differences, as follows:

• **Trade school or career college.** A local school may offer a machine shop program in which you are potentially interested. If it is a trade school, one of the advantages will be that the program can be completed in a relatively short time. Only technical or business courses will be offered, and you probably will not have to take classes outside your field of study such as English, history, or other nontechnical subjects. Upon completing the required courses, you will earn a diploma or certificate rather than a degree.

• **Two-year college.** The approach will be somewhat different at a two-year college. The term *two-year* can be somewhat misleading, for some programs can be completed in substantially less time. The term really refers to the highest level offered by a school, which in the case of two-year colleges is the associate degree.

Names of colleges of this type also can be confusing. Community colleges, junior colleges, and technical colleges can be identical in some cases but different in others. For example, in some states, technical colleges are exactly the same as community colleges. In other states, technical colleges differ in that they do not offer courses that can be transferred to four-year schools. At any rate, these differences among two-year colleges are usually insignificant for persons interested in metalworking fields. However, it may be important to establish that a school's name is truly accurate. Some trade schools refer to themselves as colleges but do not actually offer college-level work. Some others are called institutes, and in this case the school might qualify as a college or instead might actually be a trade school, depending on the type of programs offered.

What is significant is that in two-year colleges, you can pursue a more comprehensive selection of courses than in a trade school, with the end result being a college degree. To earn an associate degree, you will need to complete not only the required courses in metalworking but also some other general courses such as English composition, sociology, psychology, or history. These courses usually are transferable to four-year schools, which may not seem to matter now but may prove helpful if you ever want to pursue additional studies in the future. They also help you become a more well-rounded person and potentially a better employee.

If you are not interested in an associate degree, most two-year colleges also offer shorter programs leading to diplomas or certificates. These programs are much like those offered by trade schools, with few nontechnical courses required and no promise that credits will transfer to four-year schools.

Whether offered at the associate level or not, most two-year college programs offer the advantage of low costs. In some cases, expenses reach only a fraction of those charged by private trade schools. They may also provide a high level of respectability due to the status sometimes associated with college-level work.

Checking Out a School

To check out the features of any given school, take the following steps:

1. **Visit the school's website or obtain a copy of the school's catalog**. Check out whether it offers any programs in metalworking fields such as machining or welding and, if so, whether students earn diplomas, certificates, or associate degrees. You can often do this online by visiting a college's website.

2. **Read through the catalog**. Review information about accreditation, special programs, financial aid, and other details.

3. **Take a careful look at the catalog descriptions.** Review such details as how long it might take to complete a program and what kinds of courses are required.

4. **Study any other information you can find in the catalog or through other sources.** For example, don't overlook the course-by-course descriptions provided in most catalogs, often in the back of the publication. These summaries can let you know a great deal about the content of any program. Similarly, information on the success of graduates in obtaining jobs can prove helpful. Does the school have a career planning office? If so, that is a good sign in itself, and this office should be able to provide figures on the track record of previous students in finding jobs in their fields.

5. **Visit the school if possible.** For local schools this should not be a problem, but if you are considering going away to school, be wary of selecting a school on the basis of its publications. Every school tries to present itself in the best possible light, but you could be disappointed without a firsthand look in advance. In the process, pay attention to such factors as the condition of shops or labs and the availability of modern equipment.

6. **Look carefully at costs.** When comparing one school to the next, be sure to find out just what costs are involved. Some schools are relatively inexpensive, while others cost thousands of dollars in annual tuition and fees.

In general, schools that do not receive local or state government funding are the most costly. These include private two-year colleges, which are nonprofit, and private trade and technical schools, also known as proprietary schools, which are operated as businesses, with their main purpose to make a profit for their owners. As a result, they tend to charge significantly more than public institutions. To some extent, the extra costs can be offset by providing students with grants, scholarships, or loans. Be careful about taking loans, however; they can result in a large debt that must be paid back over a period of months or years following completion of studies. Expenses are usually much lower at public two-year colleges. Most of these schools follow an admissions policy in which anyone can attend who might benefit from an instructional program. To keep access open, they keep tuition and other costs as low as possible—usually less than $2,500 per year—and financial aid is provided for students who need assistance. From a dollar-and-cents viewpoint, the deal is hard to beat.

In addition to the cost of your course work, you will need to compare living expenses if you plan to attend school away from home. Examine the costs of rent, utilities, transportation, and food in the community where the school is located. In some cases, you may decide that although the school's rates are reasonable, the cost of living in the area is too high. Particularly for short-term programs, it is easier to attend a school close to home.

7. **Make sure the school is accredited.** Most schools are licensed by the state in which they are located, but this really means little more than that they have purchased a business license or registered with the state government. If possible, attend only a school or college that is fully accredited. A trade school, for instance, might be accredited by the Accrediting Commission of Career Schools and Colleges of Technology. A two-year college should be accredited by a regional association such as the North Central Association of Colleges and Schools or the Southern Association of Colleges and Schools.

Financing Your Training

One of the advantages of an apprenticeship or other on-the-job training is that you do not have to pay for it. Instead, you normally receive pay while the training is conducted. Even though the rate of pay probably will be lower than that of fully trained workers, this can still be a significant advantage.

Attending a trade school or two-year college is another matter. Most schools charge tuition, fees, and other costs, which can add up to a substantial total. Such costs may include the following:

- **Tuition.** This may be hundreds or even thousands of dollars, depending on the school.
- **Application fees.** These may be required before enrollment; amounts vary.
- **Books.** Costs vary; many books may be $50 to $100 each.
- **Supplies.** These may include welding rods, tools, or other necessary items.
- **Other fees.** These may include lab fees, activity fees, parking fees, and so forth.

Obtaining Financial Aid

Trade schools and colleges can be expensive. But fortunately, a great deal of financial aid is available for students who need such assistance. This includes programs offered by the government, the schools themselves, and private sources.

Applying for Financial Assistance

The key to obtaining financial assistance is to fill out the necessary application forms. Too often, students put this off until the last minute and then face delays in obtaining funds. If you need financial assistance, consult the financial aid office in a school in which you are interested and obtain the right forms. Then complete and submit them as soon as possible.

Some of the best programs available are sponsored by the U.S. government. To qualify for some of them, you must provide details about such matters as family income, assets, and debts. Although this may seem to require a lot of time and effort, the process may result in financial aid awards of hundreds or thousands of dollars, so don't be reluctant to take these steps! You probably will complete the U.S. Department of Education's Free Application for Federal Student Aid (FAFSA) plus some other forms unique to your state.

Check with a counselor to obtain the forms; they can be obtained directly from the U.S. Department of Education, from high school guidance counselors themselves, and from financial aid offices in colleges and trade schools.

Typical Student Aid Programs

Millions of students receive financial aid each year from the federal government as well as other sources to pursue postsecondary education. Some of these programs include the following:

• **Pell Grants.** These are outright grants for students. They are not loans and never have to be repaid. Eligibility is based on need, so the more help you need, the more dollars are made available.

• **Supplemental Educational Opportunity Grants (SEOG).** Like Pell Grants, these awards do not have to be repaid. A difference is that while everyone who qualifies for a Pell Grant receives one, the number of SEOG awards available at each school is limited. As a result, it is especially important to apply early for this program.

• **Special loan programs.** A number of programs provide loans to attend school, with interest rates that are lower than conventional loans due to government backing. These include Perkins Loans (previously called National Direct Student Loans), Stafford Loans (formerly known as Guaranteed Student Loans or GSLs), and PLUS loans. Some of these loans are made to parents; others are made directly to students. An advantage is that you can take a long time to repay them if desired.

• **Work-study programs.** Students in such programs earn wages by working in part-time jobs at a college or other area businesses authorized by the school.

For more information, contact the financial aid office at any school in which you're interested. Or visit the U.S. Department of Education portal at www.studentaid.gov.

In Canada, check out the government aid website for the province in which you live. Links to each site are provided by McGill University. Go to www.mcgill.ca/studentaid/government/ directory.

Some provinces participate in the Canadian Student Loan program and also offer their own aid; others administer their own student aid programs only.

In addition to government sources, you may be eligible for other assistance sponsored by the school you plan to attend, by professional organizations, or by other groups. Check with counselors or financial aid personnel for details about such programs, consult directories in libraries or bookstores, or do a Web search using terms such as "scholarships," "student aid," or "financial aid."

9

Earnings, Benefits, and Career Opportunities

The metalworking fields have much to offer in terms of pay, benefits, and varied career opportunities.

Earning Potential

Persons employed in metalworking jobs tend to earn excellent wages and benefits. Earnings vary according to a number of factors, but the following examples may illustrate the earning potential of these fields:

• Workers in the sheet-metal industry averaged more than $17 per hour in total compensation in 2004, according to the U.S. Department of Labor (DOL) as reported in the *Occupational Outlook Handbook*, 2006–2007 edition, and the top 10 percent earned more than $31 per hour.

• The median weekly wage for tool and die makers was more than $800 for the same time period, according to the Department of Labor.

• According to the DOL, median wages for welders exceed $14 per hour, and the top 10 percent earn more than $22 hourly.

• Machinists and related workers earn wages that compare favorably with other metalworking careers. Their median hourly wage exceeds $16, and many earn more than $800 a week, according to the U.S. Department of Labor.

• Jewelers and those with similar jobs average more than $27,000 annually, and some jewelers are earning more than $50,000 a year.

Through national surveys conducted in 2006, the Precision Metalforming Association has found that workers are earning salaries such as the following (with actual income fluctuating in different regions):

Inspector	$38,867
Press brake setup and operator	$39,783
Laser machine setup and operator	$40,841
Machinist	$44,044
Roll forming machine setup and operator	$44,130
CNC machine programmer	$45,503
Quality supervisor	$47,120
Production supervisor	$51,155
Maintenance group leader	$53,368
Senior tool and die maker	$55,513
Tooling supervisor	$62,539

According to Job Futures Canada (www.jobfutures.ca), sheet-metal workers earn an average hourly wage of $20.58, compared to the Canadian national average of $18.07. This pay rate is near the average for all technical, professional, and skilled occupations.

For machinists and machining and tooling inspectors in Canada, the average wage is $18.99 per hour. Canadian welders average $18.69 an hour. According to Selkirk College, those with the most training credentials and experience can exceed $100,000 per year.

It is important to realize that wages can vary a great deal depending on how long a person has worked in the field, whether the worker is a member of a trade union, and other considerations. Other factors influencing wages can include the following:

• **Unionization.** Companies that are union shops often pay higher wages than those where employees are not members of a union. In such cases, salaries and benefits are established in written agreements between the union and the employer, and they may be greater due to the union's bargaining power.

• **Location.** Workers in urban areas tend to make more than those in rural areas, and Canadian wages may be different when compared to U.S. figures due to differences in the value of currency.

• **Cost of living at the local level.** Wages can be influenced greatly by the local cost of living. In Hawaii, for instance, a gallon of milk or a house payment may cost more than twice the amount for an equivalent item in North Dakota or Alabama. Wages must, therefore, be higher to compensate for these differences.

• **National economic conditions.** The state of the national economy in Canada or the United States plays an important part in determining wages and salaries. In hard times, wages tend to increase slowly. During times of inflation wages go up more rapidly; however, so do living expenses, so don't be misled.

- **Skills required in different jobs.** Very complex metalworking jobs often pay higher wages than those requiring more basic skills. For example, workers who are trained to use computerized equipment will probably earn more than helpers who perform general duties. Also, persons in apprenticeship roles earn less than those who have moved past this status.

- **Competition.** The level of competition with other firms that employ metalworkers can have an impact on wages. This is especially true for nonunion settings. If a local company increases wages, other companies in the area may need to do the same to keep from losing workers. On the other hand, if there is little local competition, an employer may be able to get away with paying lower wages.

- **Company business conditions.** A shipbuilding company that has just won a large government contract may be able to offer high pay. A manufacturing firm that is losing money may need to reduce wages. How well a given company is doing can affect its pay scale. Similarly, a new company may have to establish itself more firmly before it is able to pay higher salaries.

Fringe Benefits

Hourly wages or monthly salaries are only part of the story. Along with basic wages, most employers offer a variety of fringe benefits to their employees. Benefits are extremely important considerations and should be examined carefully in any employment situation.

Fringe benefits can vary substantially. Factors affecting how they are determined include whether employees are unionized, whether a worker has full-time or part-time status, and patterns the employer has followed in the past.

Persons holding jobs in metalworking fields may receive benefits such as the following:

- Retirement or pension funds
- Medical insurance
- Paid vacation time
- Paid sick leave
- Worker's compensation in case of injury
- Social Security benefits
- Dental insurance
- Optical insurance
- Profit-sharing plans

In considering any job, fringe benefits should be looked at carefully along with wages themselves. An advantage of working for a large company or being a union member is that fringe benefits may be more attractive than with small companies or some nonunion employers.

Employment Prospects

Thousands of jobs become available in the metalworking industry every year. Some of these positions are needed to replace persons who retire, die, or leave the field for other jobs. Others represent new positions created as industries expand or new businesses open. The U.S. Department of Labor estimates the following numbers of persons are employed in selected metalworking fields:

Sheet-metal working	198,000
Machining and tool programming	370,000
Machine operation	1,100,000
Welding	429,000
Jewelry making	42,000
Tool and die maker	103,000

Job growth for machinists and welders is projected to be slower than average, and, in fact, the number of jobs in these two fields has declined slightly in recent years. Growth should be about the same as the average for other technical fields for sheet-metal workers. At the same time, the long-term prospects for job openings still look good in these and related fields for persons with the right training and abilities. Retirement of aging workers, as well as industrial growth, will result in substantial numbers of available jobs.

Opportunities for Women and Minorities

Most metalworking fields have been dominated by Caucasian men due to a variety of social and historical factors. However, in recent years, more and more workers from traditionally underrepresented groups have entered these fields.

Female workers, for example, now hold many jobs in metalworking. Large numbers of women first entered the workforce in the 1940s during World War II, when American and Canadian factories hired women to take the place of men who were serving in the military. Female workers played a key role in the production of war equipment, such as ships, airplanes, guns, and tanks, as well as automobiles and other domestic goods.

While many of these women left or were forced out of their jobs at the end of the war, the decades since then have seen a marked change in women's roles. Today, the idea of women workers in metalworking fields is no longer revolutionary. In fact, some employers go out of their way to hire female workers as they strive to diversify their workforce.

A similar practice is followed by many schools and colleges in recruiting students for training programs in technical fields such as metalworking. Not only do they welcome female students in such fields, but many also offer special financial aid and support programs. Examples include scholarship programs to promote gender equity or assist single parents and homemakers. Such programs may provide tuition, fees, and special counseling services. In some cases, even transportation and child-care expenses may be provided.

Members of minority racial and ethnic groups also find more opportunities than ever in metalworking fields. Hiring more members of minority groups is a common policy in many corporations and other organizations. Also, numerous scholarships and academic support programs focus on minorities. Many schools and colleges offer special grants, scholarships, counseling services, or other support for minority students.

Career Possibilities for the Disabled

Some metalworking jobs provide significant possibilities for men or women with handicaps or disabilities. Opportunities depend upon such factors as the type of disability and the extent to which it is restrictive. A person who cannot walk, for example, may not be able to function effectively as an ironworker. But the same individual may function quite well as a jeweler or as an operator of some types of metalworking machines in a workshop or factory setting.

Some employers and professional organizations offer special assistance to disabled persons. Government agencies also provide a variety of support services for the disabled ranging from training to assistance in job placement. For information on services available in your area, contact the nearest vocational rehabilitation center.

10

Planning for the Future

If you are considering a career in metalworking, plan ahead. To get yourself started in the right direction, consider such steps as the following:

- Find out exactly what training programs in metalworking fields are available in your area.
- Apply for admission to a program that seems best suited to your goals and needs.
- Visit local companies where metalworkers are employed to get a feel for the work involved.
- Talk with counselors or educators about your prospects for a career in metalworking.
- Find a job where training is provided, or start the educational program of your choice.

Locating Job Openings

Finding a job in metalworking can be accomplished in a number of ways. In some cases, the job search may take place after you have completed a training program. In others, training will be provided after you are hired. In any case, the first step is to identify job openings. To locate job openings, consult the following:

- Online job sites such as Monster.com (www.monster.com), JobWeb (www.jobweb.com), and Hot Jobs (http://hotjobs .yahoo.com)
- Company websites
- Classified advertising sections of newspapers
- Ads in business magazines that cater to metalworking professionals or other industrial personnel
- Human resource offices of companies where you would like to work
- Local employment service or job service offices
- Websites of professional associations that serve employees in metalworking fields

When you have identified an opening, you will probably have to fill out a written job application, either on paper or online. If this is required, be sure to take your time in filling it out, and answer each question completely and honestly. Be sure to double-check spelling and grammar. You can prepare ahead of time a list of your previous employers, including their names, addresses, and phone numbers; starting and ending dates of your employment; and starting and ending wage rates. Such information typically is requested on the application, and carrying a prepared list will save you from wracking your brain when you receive the application form.

Doing Well in Interviews

The next step may be to go through a job interview. If you are asked to sit for an interview, take the following steps:

• **Be prepared.** Take some time to prepare for the interview. For example, try to anticipate possible questions and practice answering them.

• **Dress neatly.** Don't make the mistake of showing up for an interview looking sloppy. Be sure to wear clean, neat clothes and present a good overall image.

• **Be on time.** Always be on time for any interview. Being late can make an employer wonder if you will have problems reporting to work on time after you are hired. In fact, it's a good idea to show up at least fifteen minutes ahead of time, in case paperwork must be completed.

• **Remain calm.** This may be easier said than done, but try to stay as calm as possible. Don't worry about possible mistakes, and just be yourself. Keep in mind that if this job does not materialize, something even better may be awaiting you.

Sooner or later, you will find that initial job. And with hard work and a positive attitude, you can be well on the way to a rewarding career in metalworking.

Schools and Colleges Offering Metalworking Programs

MANY TWO-YEAR COLLEGES offer degree, diploma, or certificate programs to train machinists, welders, and other related workers. Trade schools and career colleges also offer such programs.

Two-year, postsecondary schools may be called junior colleges, community colleges, or technical colleges. Most serve a local population, with relatively few having dormitories. This means the most convenient option is to attend a school of this type within driving distance of your home. It is possible to attend a two-year school in another city or state, but you will probably need to find an apartment or other housing on your own.

To learn what type of metalworking programs (if any) are offered by a given school or college, consult its website or catalog or contact the office of admissions.

Following is a list of some colleges and schools that offer programs in metalworking fields. This is not intended to be a complete list of all such schools but rather a sample of the institutions available. Address your correspondence to the admissions office of the school. For more details, contact a school near your home or in a location you find appealing.

In the pages following the U.S. listing is a similar list of Canadian institutions.

U.S. Institutions

Alabama

Gadsden State Community College
Gadsden, AL 35902
www.gadsdenstate.edu

George C. Wallace State Community College
Dothan, AL 36303
www.wallace.edu

John C. Calhoun State Community College
Decatur, AL 35609
www.calhoun.cc.al.us

Northwest Shoals Community College
Phil Campbell, AL 35581
www.nwscc.edu

Shelton State Community College
Tuscaloosa, AL 35404
www.sheltonstate.edu

Wallace Community College Selma
Selma, AL 36701
www.wccs.edu

Alaska

University of Alaska Southeast
Sitka, AK 99835
www.uas.alaska.edu

Arizona

Arizona Western College
Yuma, AZ 85365
www.azwestern.edu

Central Arizona College
Coolidge, AZ 85228
www.centralaz.edu

Cochise Community College
Douglas, AZ 85607
www.cochise.edu

Eastern Arizona College
Thatcher, AZ 85552
www.eac.edu

Maricopa Skill Center
Phoenix, AZ 85034
www.maricopaskillcenter.com

Pima Community College
Tucson, AZ 85709
www.pima.edu

Yavapai College
Prescott, AZ 86301
www.yc.edu

Arkansas

University of Arkansas–Fort Smith
Fort Smith, AR 72913
www.ufortsmith.edu

California

American River College
Sacramento, CA 95841
www.arc.losrios.edu

Bakersfield College
Bakersfield, CA 93305
www.bakersfieldcollege.edu

Butte College
Oroville, CA 95965
www.butte.cc.ca.us

Cerritos Community College
Norwalk, CA 90650
www.cerritos.edu

Citrus College
Glendora, CA 91741
www.citrus.cc.ca.us

College of the Redwoods
Eureka, CA 95501
www.redwoods.cc.ca.us

Compton Community Educational Center
Compton, CA 90221
www.compton.edu

De Anza College
Cupertino, CA 95014
www.deanza.edu

Fresno City College
Fresno, CA 93741
www.fresnocitycollege.edu

Long Beach City College
Long Beach, CA 90808
www.lbcc.cc.ca.us

Los Angeles Harbor College
Wilmington, CA 90744
www.lahc.edu

Los Angeles Trade-Technical College
Los Angeles, CA 90015
www.lattc.edu

Modesto Junior College
Modesto, CA 95350
www.gomjc.edu

Orange Coast College
Costa Mesa, CA 92628
www.orangecoastcollege.edu

Rio Hondo College
Whittier, CA 90601
www.riohondo.edu

San Diego City College
San Diego, CA 92101
www.sdccd.cc.ca.us

San Joaquin Delta College
Stockton, CA 95207
www.sjdccd.cc.ca.us

Yuba College
Marysville, CA 95901
www.yccd.edu

Colorado

Arapahoe Community College
Littleton, CO 80160
www.arapahoe.edu

Community College of Denver
Denver, CO 80217
www.ccd.edu

Front Range Community College
Westminster, CO 80031
www.frcc.co.us

Otero Junior College
La Junta, CO 81050
www.ojc.edu

Pikes Peak Community College
Colorado Springs, CO 80906
www.ppcc.edu

Pueblo Community College
Pueblo, CO 81004
www.pueblocc.edu

Trinidad State Junior College
Trinidad, CO 81082
www.trinidadstate.edu

Delaware

Delaware Technical and Community College
Owen Campus
Georgetown, DE 19947
www.dtcc.edu

Florida

Brevard Community College
Cocoa, FL 32922
www.brevardcc.fl.us

Central Florida Community College
Ocala, FL 34478
www.brevardcc.fl.us

Daytona Beach Community College
Daytona Beach, FL 32120
www.dbcc.fl.us

Indian River Community College
Fort Pierce, FL 34981
www.ircc.fl.us

Okaloosa-Walton College
Niceville, FL 32578
www.owcc.cc.fl.us

Santa Fe Community College
Gainesville, FL 32606
www.santafecc.fl.us

Seminole Community College
Sanford, FL 32773
www.scc-fl.edu

South Florida Community College
Avon Park, FL 33825
www.sfcc.fl.us

Georgia

Bainbridge College
Bainbridge, GA 31717
www.bainbridge.edu

Coastal Georgia Community College
Brunswick, GA 31520
www.cgcc.edu

Dalton State College
Dalton, GA 30720
www.daltonstate.edu

Darton College
Albany, GA 31707
www.darton.edu

Dekalb Technical College
Clarkston, GA 30021
www.dekalbtech.edu

Hawaii

University of Hawaii–Honolulu Community College
Honolulu, HI 96817
www.honolulu.hawaii.edu

University of Hawaii–Kauai Community College
Lihue, HI 96766
www.kauaicc.hawaii.edu

University of Hawaii–Maui Community College
Kahului, HI 96732
www.maui.hawaii.edu

Idaho

College of Southern Idaho
Twin Falls, ID 83303
www.csi.edu

East Idaho Technical College
Idaho Falls, ID 83404
www.eitc.edu

North Idaho College
Coeur D'Alene, ID 83814
www.nic.edu

Illinois

College of Du Page
Glen Ellyn, IL 60137
www.cod.edu

Danville Area Community College
Danville, IL 61832
www.dacc.cc.il.us

Elgin Community College
Elgin, IL 60123
www.elgin.edu

Highland Community College
Freeport, IL 61032
www.highland.cc.il.us

Illinois Welding School
Bartonville, Illinois 61607
www.illinoisweldingschool.com

Illinois Welding School
Romeoville, IL 60446
www.illinoisweldingschool.com

John A. Logan College
Carterville, IL 62918
www.jal.cc.il.us

John Wood Community College
Quincy, IL 62301
www.jwcc.edu

Joliet Junior College
Joliet, IL 60431
www.jjc.edu

Kankakee Community College
Kankakee, IL 60901
www.kcc.edu

Kishwaukee College
Malta, IL 60150
www.kishwaukeecollege.edu

Lewis and Clark Community College
Godfrey, IL 62035
www.lc.edu

Lincoln Land Community College
Springfield, IL 62794
www.llcc.edu

McHenry County College
Crystal Lake, IL 60012
www.mchenry.edu

Moraine Valley Community College
Palos Hills, IL 60465
www.morainevalley.edu

Oakton Community College
Des Plaines, IL 60016
www.oakton.edu

Rock Valley College
Rockford, Il 61114
www.rockvalleycollege.edu

Triton College
River Grove, IL 60171
www.triton.edu

Waubonsee Community College
Sugar Grove, IL 60554
www.wcc.cc.il.us

Indiana

Ivy Tech Community College
Evansville, IN 47710
www.ivytech.edu/evansville

Ivy Tech Community College
Fort Wayne, IN 46805
www.ivytech.edu/fortwayne

Ivy Tech Community College
Indianapolis, IN 46206
www.ivytech.edu/indianapolis

Ivy Tech Community College
Kokomo, IN 46903
www.ivytech.edu/kokomo

Ivy Tech Community College
Lafayette, IN 47903
www.laf.ivytech.edu

Vincennes University
Vincennes, IN 47591
www.vinu.edu

Iowa

Des Moines Area Community College
Ankeny, IA 50021
www.dmacc.cc.ia.us

Hawkeye Community College
Waterloo, IA 50704
www.hawkeye.cc.ia.us

Indian Hills Community College
Ottumwa, IA 52501
www.ihcc.cc.ia.us

Iowa Central Community College
Fort Dodge, IA 50501
www.icc.cc.ia.us

Iowa Western Community College
Council Bluffs, IA 51503
www.iwcc.cc.ia.us

Kirkwood Community College
Cedar Rapids, IA 52404
www.kirkwood.cc.ia.us

North Iowa Area Community College
Mason City, IA 50401
www.nia.cc.ia.us

Southeastern Community College
West Burlington, IA 52655
www.scciowa.edu

Kansas

Allen County Community College
Iola, KS 66749
www.allen.cc.edu

Barton County Community College
Great Bend, KS 67530
www.bartoncc.edu

Butler County Community College
El Dorado, KS 67042
www.butlercc.edu

Coffeyville Community College
Coffeyville, KS 67337
www.ccc.ks.us

Colby Community College
Colby, KS 67701
www.colbycc.edu

Cowley County Community College
Arkansas City, KS 67005
www.cowley.cc.ks.us

Dodge City Community and Technical College
Dodge City, KS 67801
www.dccc.ks.us

Fort Scott Community College
Fort Scott, KS 66701
www.fortscott.edu

Garden City Community College
Garden City, KS 67846
www.gccks.edu

Haskell Indian Nations University
Lawrence, KS 66046
www.haskell.edu

Hutchinson Community College
Hutchinson, KS 67501
www.hutchcc.edu

Independence Community College
Independence, KS 67301
www.indy.cc.ks.us

Johnson County Community College
Overland Park, KS 66210
www.jccc.edu

Pratt Community College
Pratt, KS 67124
www.pratt.edu

Louisiana

Bossier Parish Community College
Bossier City, LA 71111
www.bpcc.edu

Delgado Community College
New Orleans, LA 70119
www.dcc.edu

Maine

Northern Maine Technical College
Presque Isle, ME 04769
www.nmcc.edu

Maryland

Cecil Community College
North East, MD 21901
www.cecilcc.edu

Chesapeake College
Wye Mills, MD 21679
www.chesapeake.edu

Garrett College
McHenry, MD 21541
www.garrettcollege.edu

Massachusetts

North Bennet Street School
Boston, Massachusetts 02113
www.nbss.org

Michigan

Alpena Community College
Alpena, MI 49707
www.alpena.cc.mi.us

Delta College
University Center, MI 48710
www.delta.edu

Henry Ford Community College
Dearborn, MI 48128
www.hfcc.edu

Kellogg Community College
Battle Creek, MI 49017
www.kellogg.cc.mi.us

Lake Michigan College
Benton Harbor, MI 49022
www.lakemichigancollege.edu

Macomb County Community College
Warren, MI 48093
www.macomb.edu

Mid Michigan Community College
Harrison, MI 48625
www.midmichigan.edu

Monroe County Community College
Monroe, MI 48161
www.monroeccc.edu

Mott Community College
Flint, MI 48503
www.mcc.edu

Northwestern Michigan College
Traverse City, MI 49686
www.nmc.edu

Oakland Community College
Bloomfield Hills, MI 48304
www.oaklandcc.edu

Schoolcraft College
Livonia, MI 48152
www.schoolcraft.mi.cc.us

West Shore Community College
Scottville, MI 49454
www.westshore.edu

Minnesota

Dakota County Technical College
Rosemount, MN 55068
www.dctc.edu

Hennepin Technical College
Brooklyn Park, MN 55445
www.hennepintech.edu

Ridgewater College
Willmar, MN 56201
www.ridgewater.mnscu.edu

Rochester Community and Technical College
Rochester, MN 55904
www.rctc.edu

Mississippi

Coahoama Community College
Clarksdale, MS 38614
www.ccc.cc.ms.us

Copiah-Lincoln Community College
Wesson, MS 39191
www.colin.edu

East Central Community College
Decatur, MS 39327
www.eccc.cc.ms.us

Holmes Community College
Goodman, MS 39079
www.holmes.cc.ms.us

Itawamba Community College
Fulton, MS 38843
www.icc.cc.ms.us

Meridian Community College
Meridian, MS 39307
www.mcc.cc.ms.us

Mississippi Delta Community College
Moorhead, MS 38761
www.mdelta.edu

Mississippi Gulf Coast Community College
Perkinston, MS 39573
www.mgcc.edu

Northeast Mississippi Community College
Booneville, MS 38829
www.nemcc.edu

Northwest Mississippi Community College
Senatobia, MS 38668
www.northwestms.edu

Pearl River Community College
Poplarville, MS 39470
www.prcc.edu

Southwest Mississippi Community College
Summit, MS 39666
www.smcc.cc.ms.us

Missouri

Crowder College
Neosho, MO 64850
www.crowder.edu

East Central College
Union, MO 63084
www.eastcentral.edu

Jefferson College
Hillsboro, MO 63050
www.jeffco.edu

Metropolitan Community College–Longview
Lee's Summit, MO 64081
www.mcckc.edu

Moberly Area Community College
Moberly, MO 65270
www.macc.cc.mo.us

State Fair Community College
Sedalia, MO 65301
www.sfccmo.ms.us

Montana

Dawson Community College
Glendive, MT 59330
www.dawson.cc.mt.us

Flathead Valley Community College
Kalispell, MT 59901
www.fvcc.edu

Nebraska

Central Community College
Platte Campus
Columbus, NE 68601
www.cccneb.edu

Mid-Plains Community College
North Platte, NE 69101
www.mpcc.edu

Northeast Community College
Norfolk, NE 68702
www.northeastcollege.com

Western Nebraska Community College
Scotts Bluff, NE 69361
www.wncc.net

Nevada

Community College of Southern Nevada
Las Vegas, NV 89030
www.ccsn.edu

Truckee Meadows Community College
Reno, NV 89512
www.tmcc.edu

Western Nevada Community College
Carson City, NV 89703
www.wncc.edu

New Hampshire

New Hampshire Community Technical College
Berlin, NH 03570
www.berlin.nhctc.edu

New Hampshire Community Technical College
Manchester, NH 03102
www.manchester.nhct.edu

New Jersey

Middlesex County College
Edison, NJ 08837
www. middlesexcc.edu

Passaic County Community College
Paterson, NJ 07505
www.pccc.cc.nj.us

New Mexico

Clovis Community College
Clovis, NM 88101
www.clovis.edu

Eastern New Mexico University–Roswell
Roswell, NM 88202
www.roswell.enmu.edu

New Mexico Junior College
Hobbs, NM 88240
www.nmjc.edu

Northern New Mexico College
El Rito, NM 87530
www.nnmc.edu

New York

Dutchess Community College
Poughkeepsie, NY 12601
www.sunydutchess.edu

Hudson Valley Community College
Troy, NY 12180
www.hvcc.edu

Mohawk Valley Community College
Utica, NY 13501
www.mvcc.edu

Suffolk County Community College
Selden, NY 11784
www.sunysuffolk.edu

Westchester Community College
Valhalla, NY 10595
www.sunywcc.edu

North Carolina

Ashville Buncombe Technical College
Ashville, NC 28801
www.abtech.edu

Beaufort County Community College
Washington, NC 27889
www.beaufort.cc.nc.us

Caldwell Community College and Technical Institute
Hudson, NC 28638
www.caldwell.cc.nc.us

Catawba Valley Community College
Hickory, NC 28602
www.cvcc.edu

Central Piedmont Community College
Charlotte, NC 28235
www.cpcc.edu

Coastal Carolina Community College
Jacksonville, NC 28546
www.coastal.cc.nc.us

College of the Albermarle
Elizabeth City, NC 27906
www.albemarble.cc.nc.us

Forsyth Technical Community College
Winston-Salem, NC 27103
www.forsythtech.edu

Isothermal Community College
Spindale, NC 28160
www.isothermal.edu

Mitchell Community College
Statesville, NC 28677
www.mitchellcc.edu

Pitt Community College
Greenville, NC 27835
www.pitt.cc.nc.us

Randolph Community College
Asheboro, NC 27205
www.randolph.cc.nc.us

Rockingham Community College
Wentworth, NC 27375
www.rockinghamcc.edu

Southeastern Community College
Whiteville, NC 28472
www.sccnc.edu

Surry Community College
Dobson, NC 27017
www.surry.cc.nc.us

Tri-County Community College
Murphy, NC 28906
www.tccc.cc.nc.us

Wake Technical Community College
Raleigh, NC 27603
www.waketech.edu

Wilkes Community College
Wilkesboro, NC 28697
www.wilkescc.edu

North Dakota

Bismarck State College
Bismarck, ND 58506
www.bsc.nodak.edu

North Dakota State College of Science
Wahpeton, ND 58076
www.ndscs.nodak.edu

Turtle Mountain Community College
Belcourt, ND 58316
www.turtle-mountain.cc.nd.us

Ohio

Belmont Technical College
St. Clairsville, OH 43950
www.btc.edu

Columbus State Community College
Columbus, OH 43215
www.cscc.edu

Lakeland Community College
Kirkland, OH 44094
www.lakeland.cc.oh.us

Owens Community College
Toledo, OH 43699
www.owens.edu

Sinclair Community College
Dayton, OH 45402
www.sinclair.edu

Terra Community College
Fremont, OH 43420
www.tera.edu

Washington State Community College
Marietta, OH 45750
www.wscc.edu

Oklahoma

Eastern Oklahoma State College
Wilburton, OK 74578
www.eosc.edu

Murray State College
Tishomingon, OK 73460
www.msok.edu

Northeastern Oklahoma A&M College
Miami, OK 74354
www.neoam.cc.ok.us

Northern Oklahoma College
Tonkawa, OK 74653
www.north-ok.edu

Oklahoma City Community College
Oklahoma City, OK 73159
www.okc.cc.ok.us

Tulsa Community College
Tulsa, OK 74135
www.tulsacc.edu

Oregon

Blue Mountain Community College
Pendleton, OR 97801
www.bmcc.cc.or.us

Central Oregon Community College
Bend, OR 97701
www.cocc.edu

Clackamas Community College
Oregon City, OR 97045
www.clackamas.cc.or.us

Clatsop Community College
Astoria, OR 97103
www.clatsopcc.edu

Lane Community College
Eugene, OR 97405
www.lanecc.edu

Linn-Benton Community College
Albany, OR 97321
www.linnbenton.edu

Mount Hood Community College
Gresham, OR 97030
www.mhcc.edu

Portland Community College
Portland, OR 97280
www.pcc.edu

Rogue Community College
Grants Pass, OR 97527
www.roguecc.edu

Treasure Valley Community College
Ontario, OR 97914
www.tvcc.edu

Umpqua Community College
Roseburg, OR 97470
www.umpqua.edu

Pennsylvania

Community College of Allegheny County–Boyce
Monroeville, PA 15146
www.ccac.edu

Community College of Allegheny County–North
Pittsburgh, PA 15237
www.ccac.edu

Community College of Allegheny County–South
West Mifflin, PA 15122
www.ccac.edu

Community College of Beaver County
Monaca, PA 15061
www.ccbc.edu

Westmoreland County Community College
Youngwood, PA 15697
www.wccc-pa.edu

South Carolina

Aiken Technical College
Aiken, SC 29802
www.atc.edu

Central Carolina Technical College
Sumter, SC 29150
www.cctech.edu

Denmark Technical College
Denmark, SC 29042
www.denmarktech.edu

Florence Darlington Technical College
Florence, SC 29501
www.fdtc.edu

Greenville Technical College
Greenville, SC 29606
www.gvltec.edu

Horry-Georgetown Technical College
Conway, SC 29528
www.hgtc.edu

Northeastern Technical College
Cheraw, SC 29520
www.netc.edu

Orangeburg-Calhoun Technical College
Orangeburg, SC 29118
www.octech.edu

Piedmont Technical College
Greenwood, SC 29648
www.ptc.edu

Spartanburg Community College
Spartanburg, SC 29305
www.sccsc.edu

Technical College of the Lowcountry
Beaufort, SC 29902
www.tclc.edu

Tri-County Technical College
Pendleton, SC 29670
www.tctc.edu

Trident Technical College
Charleston, SC 29423
www.tridenttech.edu

York Technical College
Rock Hill, SC 29730
www.yorktech.com

Tennessee

Chattanooga State Technical Community College
Chattanooga, TN 37406
www.chattanoogastate.edu

Cleveland State Community College
Cleveland, TN 37320
www.clscc.cc.tn.us

Northeast State Technical Community College
Blountville, TN 37617
www.nstscc.cc.tn.us

Tennessee Technology Center at Harriman
Harriman, TN 37748
www.harriman.tec.tn.us

Texas

Angelina College
Lufkin, TX 75902
www.angelina.cc.tx.us

Austin Community College
Austin, TX 78752
www.austincc.edu

Brazosport College
Lake Jackson, TX 77566
www.brazosport.edu

Central Texas College
Killeen, TX 76541
www.ctcd.edu

Cisco Junior College
Cisco, TX 76437
www.cisco.cc.tx.us

Del Mar College
Corpus Christi, TX 78404
www.delmar.edu

El Paso Community College
El Paso, TX 79998
www.epcc.edu

Laredo Community College
Laredo, TX 78040
www.laredo.edu

Lee College
Baytown, TX 77522
www.leecollege.edu

Midland College
Midland, TX 79705
www.midland.edu

Mountain View College
Dallas, TX 75211
www.mountainviewcollege.edu

Navarro College
Corsicana, TX 75110
www.navarrocollege.edu

Odessa College
Odessa, TX 79764
www.odessa.edu

Paris Junior College
Paris, TX 75460
www.parisjc.edu

Ranger Junior College
Ranger, TX 76470
www.ranger.cc.tx.us

South Plains College
Levelland, TX 79336
www.southplainscollege.edu

Southwest Texas Junior College
Uvalde, TX 78801
www.swtjc.net

Tarrant County College
Fort Worth, TX 76102
www.tccd.edu

Wharton County Junior College
Wharton, TX 77488
www.wcjc.edu

Utah

College of Eastern Utah
Price, UT 84501
www.ceu.edu

Salt Lake Community College
Salt Lake City, UT 84130
www.slcc.edu

Snow College
Ephraim, UT 84627
www.snow.edu

Virginia

Central Virginia Community College
Lynchburg, VA 24502
www.cvcc.vccs.edu

Dabney S. Lancaster Community College
Clifton Forge, VA 24422
www.dl.vccs.edu

Danville Community College
Danville, VA 24541
www.dcc.vccs.edu

John Tyler Community College
Chester, VA 23831
www.jt.edu

Mountain Empire Community College
Big Stone Gap, VA 24219
www.me.vccs.edu

New River Community College
Dublin, VA 24084
www.nr.edu

Northern Virginia Community College
Annandale, VA 22003
www.nvcc.edu

Patrick Henry Community College
Martinsville, VA 24115
www.ph.vccs.edu

Southside Virginia Community College
Alberta, VA 23821
www.sv.vccs.edu

Southwest Virginia Community College
Richlands, VA 24641
www.sw.vccs.edu

Thomas Nelson Community College
Hampton, VA 23670
www.tncc.vccs.edu

Tidewater Community College
Norfolk, VA 23510
www.cvcc.vccs.edu

Virginia Western Community College
Roanoke, VA 24038
www.virginiawestern.edu

Wytheville Community College
Wytheville, VA 24382
www.wcc.vccs.edu

Washington

Big Bend Community College
Moses Lake, WA 98837
www.bigbend.edu

Centralia College
Centralia, WA 98531
www.centralia.edu

Clark College
Vancouver, WA 98663
www.clark.edu

Columbia Basin College
Pasco, WA 99301
www.columbiabasin.edu

Grays Harbor College
Aberdeen, WA 98520
www.ghc.ctc.edu

Green River Community College
Auburn, WA 98002
www.greenriver.edu

Highline Community College
Des Moines, WA 98198
www.highline.edu

Olympic College
Bremerton, WA 98337
www.olympic.edu

Shoreline Community College
Seattle, WA 98133
www.shoreline.edu

South Seattle Community College
Seattle, WA 98106
www.southseattle.edu

Walla Walla Community College
Walla Walla, WA 99362
www.wwcc.edu

West Virginia

Southern West Virginia Community and Technical College
Logan, WV 25637
www.southern.wvnet.edu

Wisconsin

Fox Valley Technical College
Appleton, WI 54913
www.fvtc.edu

Lakeshore Technical College
Cleveland, WI 53015
www.gotoltc.edu

Madison Area Technical College
Madison, WI 53704
www.matcmadison.edu

Milwaukee Area Technical College
Milwaukee, WI 53233
www.matc.edu

Waukesha County Technical College
Pewaukee, WI 53072
www.wtct.edu

Western Technical College
La Crosse, WI 54602
www.westerntc.edu

Wyoming

Casper College
Casper, WY 82601
www.caspercollege.edu

Central Wyoming College
Riverton, WY 82501
www.cwc.edu

Eastern Wyoming College
Torrington, WY 82240
www.ewc.wy.edu

Western Wyoming Community College
Rock Springs, WY 82902
www.wwcc.wy.edu

Canadian Institutions

Alberta

Lakeland College
Fort Kent, AB T0A 1H0
www.lakeland.edu

Northern Alberta Institute of Technology
Edmonton, AB T5G 2R1
www.nait.edu

Southern Alberta Institute of Technology
Calgary, AB T2M 0L4
www.sait.edu

British Columbia

British Columbia Institute of Technology
Burnaby, BC V5G 3H2
www.bcit.edu

Camosun College Lansdowne Campus
Victoria, BC V8Z 4C4
www.camosun.edu

College of New Caledonia
Prince George, BC V2N 1P8
www.cnc.bc.ca

College of the Rockies
Cranbrook, BC V1C 5L7
www.cotr.bc.ca

Kwantlen University College
Surrey, BC V3W 2M8
www.kwantlen.bc.ca

North Island College
Courtenay, BC V9N 8N6
www.nic.bc.ca

Selkirk College
Castlegar, BC V1N 3J1
www.selkirk.ca

Thompson Rivers University
Kamloops, BC V2C 5N3
www.tru.ca

University College of the Fraser Valley
Abbotsford, BC V2S 7M9
www.ucfv.ca

Manitoba

Keewatin Community College
The Pas, MB R9A 1M7
www.keewatincc.mb.ca

Red River College
Winnipeg, MB R3H 0J9
www.rrc.mb.ca

Winnipeg Technical Centre
Winnipeg, MB R3Y 1G5
www.wtc.mb.ca

New Brunswick

College Communautaire du Nouveau Brunswick
Ministre de l'enseignement superieur et du travail
Fredericton, NB E3B 5H1
www.nbcc.nb.ca

Newfoundland

College of the North Atlantic
St-John's, NF
www.cna.nl.ca

Northwest Territories

Aurora College
Fort Smith, NT X0E 0P0
www.auroracollege.nt.ca

Nova Scotia

Cape Breton University
Sydney, NS B1P 6L2
www.cnc.bc.ca

Nova Scotia Community College
Halifax, NS B3J 2X1
www.nscc.ns.ca

Ontario

Algonquin College of Applied Arts and Technology
Woodroffe Campus
Nepean, ON K2G 1V8
www.algonquin.on.ca

Confederation College of Applied Arts and Technology
Thunder Bay Campus
Thunder Bay, ON P7C 4W1
www.confederation.on.ca

Conestoga College of Applied Arts and Technology
Conestoga Campus
Kitchener, ON N2G 4M4
www.conestoga.on.ca

Fanshawe College of Applied Arts and Technology
London Campus
London, ON N5W 5H1
www.fanshawe.on.ca

Fleming College
Sutherland Campus
Peterborough, ON K9J 7B1
www.flemingc.on.ca

George Brown College of Applied Arts and Technology
Toronto, ON M5T 2T9
www.georgebrown.on.ca

Georgian College
Barrie, ON L4M 3X9
www.georgianc.on.ca

Georgian College of Applied Arts and Technology
Barrie Campus
Barrie, ON L4M 3X9
www.georcollege.on.ca

Lambton College of Applied Arts and Technology
Sarnia, ON N7S 6K4
www.lambton.on.ca

Niagara College
Welland, ON L3B 5S2
www.niagaracollege.on.ca

Northern College of Applied Arts and Technology
Porcupine Campus
Timmins, ON P4N 8R6
www.northern.on.ca

Sault College of Applied Arts and Technology
Sault Sainte Marie, ON P6A 5L3
www.sault.on.ca

Seneca College of Applied Arts and Technology
Willowdale, ON M2J 2X5
www.seneca.on.ca

Sheridan Institute of Technology and Advanced Learning
Oakville, ON L6H 2L1
www.sheridaninstitute.ca

Prince Edward Island

Holland College
Charlottetown, PE C1A 4Z1
www.hollandc.on.ca

Saskatchewan

Saskatchewan Institute of Applied Sciences and Technology
Saskatoon, SK S7K 5X2
www.sias.sk.ca

Appendix B

Selected Organizations Related to Metalworking

American Machine Tool Distributors' Association
1445 Research Blvd.
Rockville, MD 20850
www.amtda.org

American Welding Society
55 Northwest Le Jeune Rd.
Miami, FL 33126
www.aws.org

ASM International (The Materials Information Society)
9639 Kinsman Rd .
Materials Park, OH 44073
www.asminternational.org

Associated General Contractors of America Inc.
2300 Wilson Blvd., Ste. 400
Arlington, VA 22201
www.agc.org

Canadian Association of Moldmakers
St. Clair College
2000 Talbot Rd. West, Box #16
Windsor, ON N9A 6S4
www.camm.ca

Canadian Institute of Steel Construction (CISC-ICCA)
201 Consumers Rd., Ste. 300
Willowdale, ON M2J 4G8
www.cisc-icca.ca

Canadian Sheet Steel Building Institute
652 Bishop St. North
Cambridge, ON N3H 4V6
www.cssbi.ca

Canadian Tooling and Machining Association
140 McGovern Dr., Unit #3
Cambridge, ON N3H 4R7
www.ctma.com

International Association of Machinists and Aerospace Workers
900 Machinists Pl.
Upper Marlboro, MD 20772
www.goiam.org

International Association of Machinists and Aerospace
   Workers (Canada)
15 Gervais Dr., Ste. 707
North York, ON M3C 1Y8
www.iamaw.ca

Jewelers of America
52 Vanderbilt Ave., 19th Fl.
New York, NY 10017
www.jewelers.org

Metal Building Contractors and Erectors Association
P.O. Box 499
Shawnee Mission, KS 66201
www.mbcea.org

National Institute for Metalworking Skills
10565 Fairfax Blvd., Ste. 203
Fairfax, VA 22030
www.nims-skills.org

National Ornamental and Miscellaneous Metals Association
1535 Pennsylvania Ave.
McDonough, GA 30253
www.nomma.org

National Tooling and Machining Association
9300 Livingston Rd.
Fort Washington, MD 20744
www.ntma.org

North American Die Casting Association
241 Holbrook Dr.
Wheeling, IL 60090-5809
www.diecasting.org

Precision Machined Products Association
6700 W. Snowville Rd.
Brecksville, OH 44141
www.pmpa.org

Precision Metalforming Association
6363 Oak Tree Blvd.
Independence, OH 44131-2500
www.pma.org

Precision Metalforming Association Educational Foundation
6363 Oak Tree Blvd.
Independence, OH 44131-2500
www.metalforming.com/edufound

Sheet Metal and Air Conditioning Contractors' National Association
4201 Lafayette Center Dr.
Chantilly, VA 20151
www.smacna.org

Sheet Metal Workers' International Association
1750 New York Ave. NW
Washington, DC 20006
www.smwia.org

Sheet Metal Workers' International Association
190 Thames Rd. East
Exeter, ON N0M 1S3
www.smwia.org

Tooling and Manufacturing Association
1177 S. Dee Rd.
Park Ridge, IL 60008
www.tmanet.com

Further Reading

Bennett, Scott. *The Elements of Résumé Style: Essential Rules and Eye-Opening Advice for Writing Résumés and Cover Letters That Work.* AMACOM, 2005.

Bone, Jan. *Opportunities in Laser Technology Careers.* McGraw-Hill, 2008.

Codina, Carles. *The Complete Book of Jewelry Making: A Full-Color Introduction to the Jeweler's Art.* Lark Books, 2006.

Gisler, Margaret, and Marjorie Eberts. *Careers for Hard Hats and Other Constructive Types.* McGraw-Hill, 2001.

Harvey, James. *Machine Shop Trade Secrets: A Guide to Manufacturing Machine Shop Practices.* Industrial Press, 2005.

Hu, Jack, Zdzislaw Marciniak, and John Duncan (editors). *Mechanics of Sheet Metal Forming.* Butterworth-Heinemann, 2005.

Krar, Steve, Arthur Gill, Peter Smid, and Paul Wanner. *Machine Tool Technology Basics.* Industrial Press, 2003.

Lareau, Viki. *Marketing and Selling Your Handmade Jewelry: The Complete Guide to Turning Your Passion into Profit.* Interweave Press, 2006.

McCauley, Christopher, and Edward Hoffman. *Shop Reference for Students and Apprentices, from Machinery's Handbook.* Industrial Press, 2001.

Résumés for High-Tech Careers. McGraw-Hill, 2003.

Rowh, Mark. *Careers for Crafty People and Other Dexterous Types.* McGraw-Hill, 2006.

Smid, Peter. *CNC Programming Handbook.* Industrial Press, 2002.

Sumichrast, Michael. *Opportunities in Building Careers.* McGraw-Hill, 2007.

U.S. Department of Labor. *Occupational Outlook Handbook,* 2007–2008.

Walker, John R., and W. Richard Polanin. *ARC Welding.* Goodheart-Willcox, 2004.

About the Author

MARK ROWH IS an educator and writer who specializes in career, education, and business topics. His higher education experience has included administrative positions at New River Community College (Virginia), Greenville (South Carolina) Technical College, Bluefield (West Virginia) State College, and Parkersburg (West Virginia) Community College. In these positions, Rowh has worked closely with a variety of occupational programs. He holds a doctorate in vocational and technical education from Clemson University.

Rowh's articles have appeared in more than sixty magazines. He has contributed to a number of other books published by McGraw-Hill including *Opportunities in Electronics Careers* and *Great Jobs for Chemistry Majors.*